D1598753

A
COLLECTOR'S
PICTORIAL BOOK
OF
BAYONETS

1. General Sir Geoffrey Baker inspecting troops at Colchester Garrison in June 1969. The bayonets seen in this photograph are the current British issue bowie-bladed L13A. A feature of distinction on these bayonets is the enlarged muzzle ring: the necessity of this feature to enable the bayonet to fit over the flash-eliminator is clearly illustrated in the photograph. *Colchester Express*

A
COLLECTOR'S
PICTORIAL BOOK
OF
BAYONETS

by

Frederick J. Stephens

STACKPOLE BOOKS

Published in the U.S.A.
in 1971, by
STACKPOLE BOOKS,
Cameron and Kelker Streets,
Harrisburg, Pa. 17105

SBN 8117–0384–3

Library of Congress Catalog Card number 71–144108

To Joyce, my wife,
and to
Nicole, my daughter

Printed in Great Britain

Contents

Acknowledgements

I am greatly indebted to my many friends, colleagues, acquaintances and pen-friends who have so unstintingly aided me. This work is a tribute to their interest and aid.

I particularly wish to express my heartfelt thanks to Roger D. C. Evans without whose interest and friendship this book would never have been completed. Gratitude is also due to George Seymour, of S & G Arms, who so patiently permitted the author to invade the tranquility of his home armed with camera, tripod and all the necessary paraphernalia.

Sincere thanks go also to Mr. Roy Butler and staff of Wallis & Wallis; the authorities of the Tower of London; Dave and Jackie Hillman; Mr. Douglas A. Nie and the staff of Weller & Dufty Ltd.; Herman A. Maeurer; Ken Holdich; J. B. Marsh; J. Anthony Carter; Jan Pieter Puype; M. H. Cole; Ivor F. Bush; John Burden; Tony L. Oliver; Brian L. Davis; Hugh Page Taylor; Dr. John Kennaugh; R. J. Wilkinson-Latham; the Department of the Army, Washington USA; the *Colchester Express*; and to my old colleague Paul Tyrrell, who produced such excellent results from my ham-fisted negatives.

Finally my thanks to Trevor and Yvonne, who supplied endless cups of coffee and helped with the typing.

Frederick J. Stephens

Introduction

More money has probably been expended by mankind in the pursuit of the 'ultimate deterrent' than in achieving any other single goal. To a generation whose daily lives are never far removed from the nuclear weapons possessed by several of today's nations and whose eyes and ears are constantly assailed by news of new developments both in chemical and biological warfare the bayonet may seem an anachronism, long since stripped of any practical value. After all, it may be argued, the origins of the bayonet lie several centuries past and one can hardly compare Marlborough's campaigns of the early years of the eighteenth century with the present Vietnam conflict. Why then should the bayonet have survived so long? It is noticeable that few modern armies have discarded such weapons: the British Army adopted the L1A1 bayonet with the FN-designed rifle and the American forces still use the M7 bayonet on the M16. A survey of most armies reveals that most retain bayonets in some form or another.

History and Design

The initial improvisation, so legend has it, occurred in desperation, when knives were thrust into musket muzzles as a last resort: the dates ascribed to this are vague but the armies of the seventeenth century were quick to realise the value of such a weapon when coupled with the limited efficiency of their match- and flintlock muskets. This continued through two centuries, as little improvement was made to the guns in this period and the bayonet was still a very useful asset. Towards the beginning of the Crimean War—an era much noted for resplendent uniforms and a total disregard for camouflage—the bayonet came to be regarded as an attractive accessory to the uniform and a whole range of brass-hilted or brass-mounted sabre bayonets appeared and replaced the archaic socket type. These weapons certainly looked effective, but it may be argued that their moral value was far greater than their physical effects! Towards the end of the nineteenth century the knife bayonet appeared, perhaps the best known examples being the German Seitengewehr M-71/84 and the Austrian Mannlicher series of 1886–95—although the American Dahlgren bayonet of 1861 is a serious contender for the title of the first true knife bayonet.

The Boer War forced home the realisation that the idea of chivalry in war was fast vanishing, and the sodden trenches of the Somme and

8

Passchendaele killed the myth completely. The trenches of the Great War saw great activity as the battles surged first one way and then the other —but, in the bitter hand-to-hand fighting that occasionally raged, the bayonet was again found to be of little use, being too long and unwieldy. This was particularly noticeable on the German side where the *frontschweine* —experienced soldiers who had survived earlier engagements—used sharpened shovels, automatic pistols and 'trench knives', (with short double edged blades) in preference to their bayonets.

In the inter-war years, the British Army carried out a considerable series of tests to determine the effectiveness of the Pattern 1907 sword bayonet. It was—they decided—too long, too heavy, far from ideal as a killing weapon or wood-chopper, reflected the light even though dulled and was comparatively useless as a hand weapon. Their recommendations brough back the socket bayonet under the guise of the 'Spike bayonet, No. 4 Mk. I', which was totally useless for any purpose except stabbing and became much disliked by the troops. World War II suspended much of such experimentation but the future of the bayonet was shown by the American adoption of the M4 knife bayonet in May 1944, a derivative— albeit ill-balanced—of the M3 knife. The post-war armies have, almost without exception, adopted knife bayonets (generally wholly or partly double-edged) with blades between 6″ and 9″ long and few developments seem likely to attain widespread issue in the next few years.

It is possible that the end of the bayonet is in sight, as the current trend towards hand-held missile systems and similar impedimenta may eventually relegate the bayonet to museums and collectors' show cases. Conversely, however, the demise of the cartridge firearm is far from predictable and, with a general need for a utility knife, the bayonet may be retained as an ancillary weapon for many years yet.

Collecting

The collecting of bayonets has only come to be regarded as bona fide within the last few years although, even now, it has yet to receive the attention devoted, for example, to flintlock firearms. It is also still relatively inexpensive—although prices are rising rapidly—and a good basic collection can be amassed for a limited outlay.

Most novice collectors, although there are a few exceptions, start by trying to obtain 'one of everything' with little regard for style, period or type. Many, however, go past this stage and attempt to specialize either on a particular country—usually Germany or Great Britain—or on a particular period. It has been known that some collectors have confined themselves solely to the variations encountered in a single type of bayonet, the Canadian Ross and the Japanese Arisaka being given as examples.

Before a collector begins to specialize some knowledge of the various patterns and models is essential, and it is with this idea in mind that this book has been written. I decided to restrict myself to bayonets I had been able to examine, with occasional reference to known variations: I have avoided a real study of the weapon's origin as this in itself would merit a complete volume. The work is mainly concerned with bayonets produced during the nineteenth and twentieth centuries—the heyday of the bayonet. Specimens from the seventeenth and eighteenth centuries have not been totally ignored, but this was an era of plug and socket bayonets which generally resemble each other in all but detail. From a collector's point of view, such early weapons are not generally available and the many patterns that abounded between 1800 and 1945 represent the most challenging field. Within this period some strange experiments and bizarre ideas appeared alongside bayonets of more traditional form. This, then, is a basic manual for the collector.

Nomenclature

An important feature in the study of the bayonet, and indeed in the study of any realm of collecting, is a comprehensive understanding of the basic subject. The greater the appreciation of this fact, then the greater the appreciation of the knowledge that becomes available to the student. It has been my consideration of this that has prompted me not to devote much space to the early history of.the bayonet but to apply some of these pages to a description of the various parts. By this it is not meant to imply that a study of the early history of the bayonet is of little use, it is more a proper acknowledgement that such information is of greater value to the more specialist student and that, generally speaking, this book will be for the use of the general collector and layman.

Having indulged in a fascination for edged weapons since my schooldays, with particular emphasis on the bayonet in recent years, I am privileged to have had the opportunity to meet fellow collectors, visit innumerable collections and discuss relative details with fellow authors. From the various contacts made and numerous books and publications studied—especially those that have made some degree of study available to the bayonet collector—I have noted that, of all the books on bayonets that are available, few have made a really serious effort at describing the nomenclature of a bayonet.

Perhaps this situation is not altogether surprising, for to form an accurate and comprehensive guide is indeed a study in itself, so numerous and varied are different patterns. I have therefore taken pains to provide for this reference a nomenclature that will, at least, give the reader a working knowledge of the subject. It would be fatuous to pretend that this section of the book is the ultimate study in bayonet construction, but it is a beginning. I am sure that there is information here that will have great appeal to the specialist student, just as much as to the novice: I hope both may benefit from its inclusion.

11

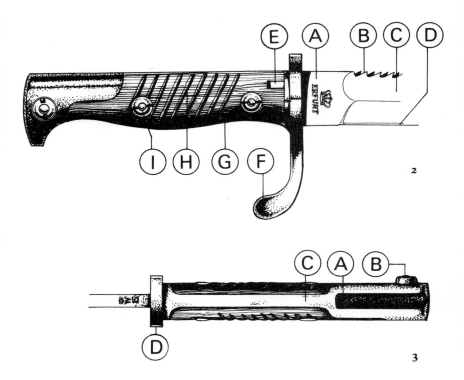

Drawings by John Walter.

2. Details of the hilt of a knife bayonet, in this case a German sawback. Distinctly seen are: A—the trademark on the ricasso; B—serrations; C—fuller; D—edge; E—oiling hole; F—quillon (up-swept); G—grips; H—grip grooving; I—securing bolts and nuts.

3. The back of the hilt, showing: A—mortise slot; B—press stud; C—tang; D—half-barrel ring.

12

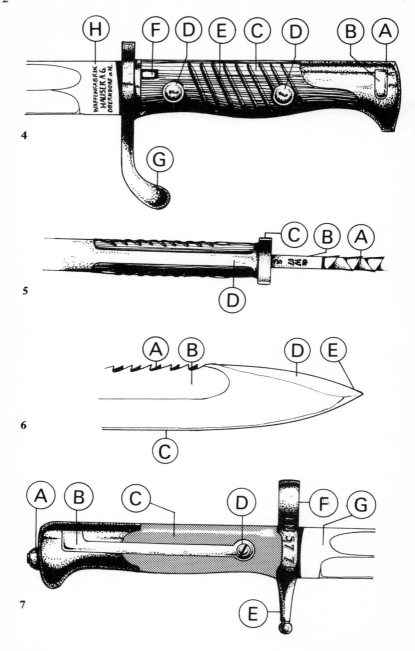

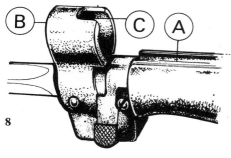

8

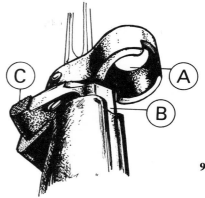

9

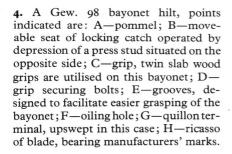

4. A Gew. 98 bayonet hilt, points indicated are: A—pommel; B—moveable seat of locking catch operated by depression of a press stud situated on the opposite side; C—grip, twin slab wood grips are utilised on this bayonet; D—grip securing bolts; E—grooves, designed to facilitate easier grasping of the bayonet; F—oiling hole; G—quillon terminal, upswept in this case; H—ricasso of blade, bearing manufacturers' marks.

5. A detail view of the back of Gew. 98 bayonet. Points to observe are: A—serrations; B—back of blade without serration which bears the markings 'Crown over W 07' (the latter being the year of manufacture—1907); C—half-barrel ring; D—tang of blade.

6. The tip of the blade of the previously illustrated bayonet, showing: A—serrations; B—fuller; C—edge of blade; D—False-edge; E—point.

7. A Vetterli-Vitali bayonet hilt, points marked are: A—tang projection, bossed over and secured at the pommel head; B—locking catch spring, activated by

depression of a press stud situated on the opposite side of the pommel. The principle of fixture is similar to that of the Gew. 98 described, except that in this case the spring is exterior fitted, and on the Gew. 98 it is an interior fitting; C—grip; D—securing screw, holding both spring and grip in position; E—quillon terminal, in this case the original downswept quillon has been removed, and the end rounded off; F—quillon containing barrel ring; G—ricasso of blade.

8. A close-up of the hilt of a French Lebel bayonet, showing: A—mortise slot for the rifle bayonet lug; B—barrel ring; C—foresight recess.

9. A view showing the Lebel hilt: A—barrel ring; B—locking clip; C—press catch integral with B.

14

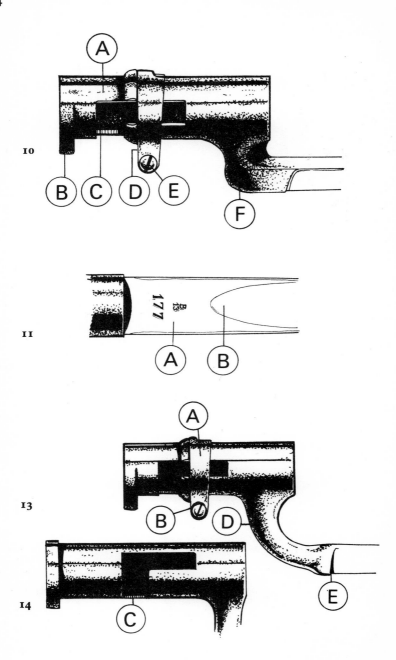

10

11

13

14

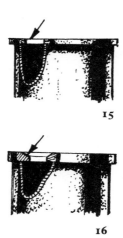

15

16

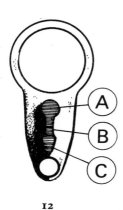

12

10. A socket bayonet hilt, showing the component parts: A—socket; B—foresight lip; C—foresight slot; D—locking ring; E—tightening screw (controls rigidity of locking ring); F—elbow.

11. A slightly different view of the same socket, showing: A—upper surface of blade; B—fuller.

12. A close-up of a bowie bladed bayonet with blade cut in half. Note the formation of the blade: A—thickened back edge; B—recesses of fullers; C—contour of edge.

13, 14. Two socket bayonet hilts, the upper that of a Three-band Enfield bayonet, the lower that of a Kukri socket bayonet. The features marked on the illustration are: A—foresight locking ring; B—tightening screw on locking ring; C—foresight slot; D—elbow; E—shoulder.

15, 16. A close-up view of two scabbard throats, showing differences in lip formation.

17   18   19

17. A European plug bayonet, possibly of German manufacture. The straight blade tapers to a double-edged point, while the tang passes up through the wooden grip and is secured to the latter at the pommel. Both the hilt fittings and the finial are brass. Blade length 12″: overall length 17″. *S & G Arms*

18. A European plug bayonet, *c.* 1680. The blade is broad and spear-like in shape and is surmounted by two straight quillons. Both the ferrule and finial are made of steel, as are the quillons and blade. The grip is black polished wood, drilled through to accommodate the tang which was then bossed over. Blade length 9½″: overall length 16″. *R. D. C. Evans*

19. An English plug bayonet, *c.* 1680. The grip of this bayonet is made of wood, turned and drilled through the centre to accommodate the tang of the blade: the pommel consists of a metal cap, through which the tang projects and is bossed over.

A steel ferrule terminates the grip and a steel crosspiece, with double quillons —one set hooked—form the guard of the bayonet.

The blade of this piece is especially interesting, as it has been manufactured from a triangular sword blade. Examination of the bayonet indicates that the assembly of this piece was contemporary with the estimated date of manufacture. It was not uncommon during the era of the plug bayonet to utilise a broken sword blade as a bayonet blade. The illustrated example is a fine specimen of such practice. *R. D. C. Evans*

20. A European plug bayonet, possibly of English or German manufacture, *c.* 1700. This is a sporting bayonet, the blade being engraved with floral motifs and a leaping wolf—such embellishments being characteristic of this type of weapon rather than those of military

20

pattern. The grip is made of wood and the hilt fittings are of brass. The blade is fitted by having the tang project through the grip, and bossed over at the pommel. A brass finial fits over the pommel and adds the finishing touch of quality to this fine bayonet. *Wallis & Wallis.*

18

21   22   23

24

25

26

21. An example of the split-socket bayonet, a rare and short-lived invention that preceded the introduction of the socket bayonet. It is believed that the French were the first to produce bayonets of this pattern—in about 1671—the design being an improvement of the ring bayonet. The split-socket bayonet was intended to fit barrels of varying diameter; the socket was made with a longitudinal split which allowed expansion or contraction of the tube so that it could be securely attached to the muzzle of the musket. The example illustrated has a shell guard formed on the shoulder to serve the same purpose as a quillon—to foil an adversary's blade in combat. The blade is tapered, and double-edged for about five inches along the lower portion. Blade lengths of these items varied. The example shown is probably English or French manufacture, *c.* 1700. Blade length 12″. *S & G Arms*

22, 23. Two further views of the split-socket bayonet, showing the formation of the shell guard on the shoulder directly over the blade, and the split in the socket extending from the foresight slot to the end of the tube.

24, 25, 26. Three early 18th century socket bayonets; a sword/socket bayonet of all steel manufacture with a cruciform hilt, the blade is straight and double-edged. A sporting socket bayonet, the removable grip of which permits use of the bayonet as a short hunting sword: this bayonet is most unusual and has a knuckle bow incorporated in the hilt design, the pommel is chiselled in relief and the broad curved blade is unfullered. A 'zig-zag' bayonet with straight unfullered blade, a shell guard is incorporated in the shoulder of the socket—designed to foil an opponent's blade in combat. *Tower of London collection, Crown copyright.*

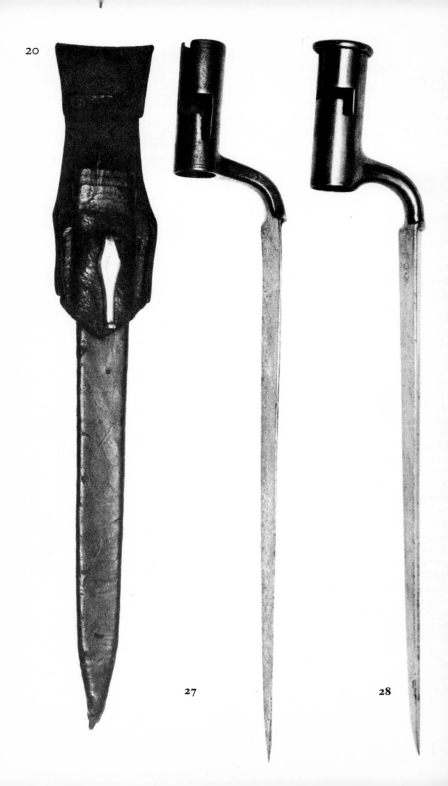

20
27
28

27. An English socket bayonet, *c.* 1720. The scabbard is brown leather, with a leather frog secured by a brass frog stud. The blade is triangular in cross-section, though of such dimensions that only two edges are suitable cutting edges. Blade length 17″. *S & G Arms*

28. The introduction, about 1700, of the socket bayonet as a standard service accoutrement for muskets brought about an accepted standard design for British bayonets. The various experiments previously effected with the *bayonette* had resulted in the production of many varied patterns, the results of which are today an unending source of difficulty for the collector faced with the identification of such pieces.

The earlier examples of the socket bayonet (1700–1750) tend to be distinctive in having a broad, flat, unfullered blade. The design was modified in about 1750, when the shape of the blade became slightly curved and triangular in cross-section, fullered on two faces of the blade. With some modifications, this continued to be the style of English socket bayonets right up to the Pattern 1853 Enfield socket bayonet. There have, of course, been exceptions to this general rule, but these are discussed in later pages.

The socket bayonet illustrated is a cadet bayonet pattern of 1750. The shortest of all British socket bayonets made for military use, the blade length is 9″. A socket bayonet with an 11″ blade was made for Sergeants of the Line, but the most commonly encountered British bayonet of this period is the standard type issued to all ranks with a 15″ blade. *S & G Arms*

29. An English Volunteer bayonet, *c.* 1750. This socket bayonet displays a rather unusual locking device which operates by means of a clip spring placed on the socket. The blade is straight, double-edged, and unfullered, having the blade construction of knife pattern,

29

rather than the more popular triangular cross-section. No scabbard was made for this piece: when not in use it was carried in a compartment cut into the butt of the gun.

Overall length approx. 12″. *S & G Arms*

22

30

31

32

33

34

30. The British Brown Bess Land Pattern bayonet, with metal scabbard.

The illustrated example has a distinctive locking spring clip situated on the socket, and is believed to have been used by the East India Company troops. The socket is browned and the scabbard painted black. *S & G Arms*

31, 32. A socket bayonet for the East India Company, *c.* 1800. This bayonet is identifiable by the heart-shaped mark containing the letters VEIC, and was in use until about 1805. The bayonet is of English manufacture and the side of the socket is fitted with a spring catch, intended to lock around the foresight of the musket in a fixed position.

The blade is straight, unfullered and triangular in cross-section, only two of the sides having cutting edges. *S & G Arms*

33. An exercise in bayonet practice, detailed from *Relatorio da Escola Central de Tiro* (Portuguese Army Training Manual, 1856).

34. A second exercise in bayonet practice, detailed from *Relatorio da Escola Central de Tiro.*

24

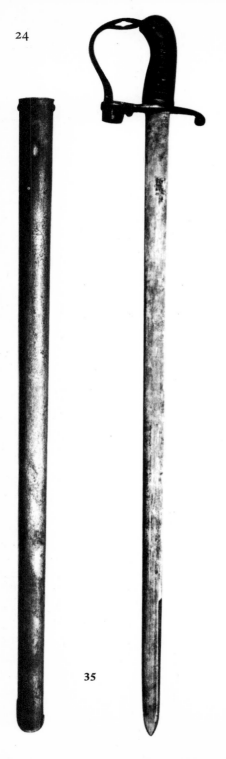

35. A volunteer bayonet, *c.* 1797. This sword/socket bayonet was first produced for use with a Staudenmeyer volunteer rifle and both the gun and the bayonet were adopted by a number of Volunteer Regiments—among them the London and Westminster Light Horse Volunteers. The steel hilt is inset with a wire bound contoured wooden grip and both the knuckle-bow and crosspiece have fittings to receive the rifle barrel. The blade is straight, single-edged (double-edged at tip) and unfullered. The scabbard is steel, with screw fittings at the throat and an oval frog stud while the tip has a small drag. A number of scabbards for this pattern of bayonet have been noted to be marked JOHNSTONES, SWORD CUTLERS and it is possible that this concern was the sole manufacturer of these pieces. It is unfortunate that the manufacturer did not give further details about himself or his premises, as a number of sword cutlers by the name of Johnston worked within the boundaries of the City of London: the most probable of these firms, assuming the bayonet was manufactured between 1797 and 1800, would be Joshua Johnston, of 8 Newcastle St., Strand, or Richard Johnston and Robert Foster of 68 St James St. Blade length 30⅜": overall length 35". *S & G Arms*

35

36

36. A Prussian Hirschfängeꝛ bayonet, c. 1790, for an unidentified Jäger rifle. Variation patterns are encountered, with such distinct features as knuckle-bows. The hilt is of brass and contains a spring fitting; the blade is single edged. Blade length 19⅝"; overall length 24½". *R. D. C. Evans*

37. A volunteer sword/socket bayonet, c. 1800. Although sword/socket bayonets are, in general, quite scarce, they usually display manufacture far superior to the standard regimental patterns. Volunteer and yeomanry regiments had an advantage over the rank and file of British regiments in that they were permitted to design and purchase their own bayonets —a privilege not shared by regular regiments. The only regulation governing volunteer bayonets was that all those used by a regiment were to be identical. As various volunteer regiments had additional finances with which to supplement their arms purchases, an interesting variety of volunteer bayonets can be encountered, the majority of which exist in combinations of the sword/socket pattern.

The bayonet illustrated is of all-steel construction, the socket tube being intended as the sword grip. An interesting feature of this particular item is that no provision is made in the socket for securing the bayonet to the rifle. No allowance is made for the foresight of the gun, nor is there any locking ring with which to secure the bayonet. The blade is straight and single-edged, (double-edged at the tip) and fullered on both sides. Blade length 22": overall length 26½". *S & G Arms*

38. An unidentified Baker pattern bayonet which has the unusual feature of a five-ball crosspiece and a five-ball knuckle bow. Although no information on this piece is yet available to identify it, it is thought to be a specially made volunteer pattern. *Weller & Dufty.*

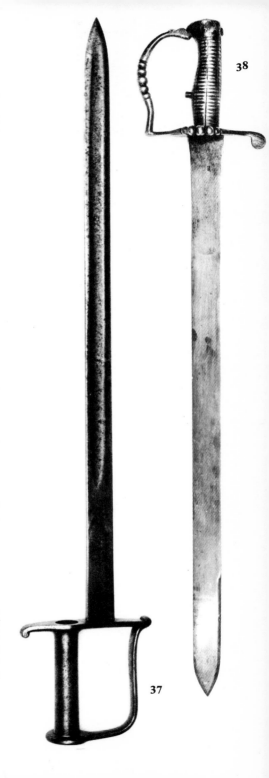

38

37

26

39 40 41

39. The First Pattern Baker bayonet, 1800. The first issue Baker bayonets were similar in design to a brass stirrup-hilted sword. Manufactured by Osborne of Birmingham, the design of the bayonet is not unlike that of a German hunting sword—which is not too surprising, since the design of the Baker rifle was copied from that of the German *Jäger* rifle. The scabbard for the bayonet is black leather with brass fittings. *S & G Arms*

40. The Second Pattern bayonet for the Baker rifle, introduced in 1801 and remaining in service until about 1815. Similar to the preceding pattern, it differed primarily in having a curved knuckle-bow. Locking was achieved by means of a spring and groove cut into the reverse of the hilt. *S & G Arms*

41. A Brown Bess type socket bayonet, manufactured by Henry Nock, *c*. 1810.

The most interesting feature of this bayonet is the unfinished floral engraving displayed on the face of the blade. The bayonet itself is of standard Brown Bess form, but the decoration of the blade may indicate that it may have been intended for presentation.

The fact that this ornamentation is unfinished is of particular interest, as the method of decoration of blades can be clearly observed. The design was in the first instance engraved on to the blade and the background area then removed to bring the decoration into relief. No information is available about the origin of this particular piece, so it may well have been a test piece of engraving attempted by an apprentice armourer. *S & G Arms*

42. The Baker experimental hand bayonet, *c*. 1819. In 1819 the British Government factory at Enfield undertook the conversion of 500 Baker rifles to a new pattern. A bayonet was required for this new pattern, and as an experiment 560 bayonets (which had been intended for

42

Nock's 'Duke of Richmond' musket), then regarded as obsolete, were altered to fit the new Baker pattern. The modification was really a Baker hilt fitted with a Nock socket bayonet blade. Blade length 8½″: overall length 13″. *S & G Arms*

28

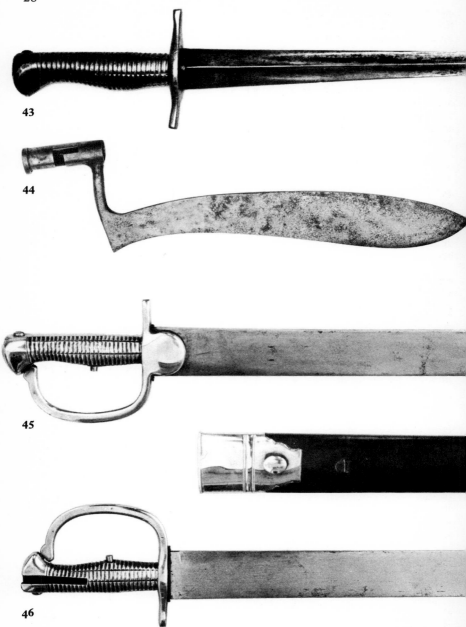

43

44

45

46

43. The First Pattern hand bayonet—or Fourth Pattern Baker bayonet—1823. Following the first modifications to the Baker rifle in 1819, a contract was placed for the modification of all full-stocked Baker rifles. The bayonets to be used with this were again modified but, instead of utilising obsolete Nock bayonet blades, full-length socket bayonet blades were adopted with a modified version of the Second Pattern Baker bayonet hilt. Blade length 20½″: overall length 25¼″. *S & G Arms*

44. It has been rumoured in recent years that a bayonet, conforming the design of a Kukri knife but bearing a socket fitting, was used by Indian troops during the period 1820–40. There has been no conclusive information to prove, or disprove this, except the existence of some bayonets which appear to resemble a Kukri knife more than a bayonet. The illustrated piece is one such item.

It can be reasonably argued that this bayonet is not a Kukri *per se*, for it has a number of features absent on Kukri knives. The most striking of these is that the cutting edge is on the back of the blade, and the false edge on the lower. *It has been observed that socket fittings, to which have been attached Kukri blades, have been manufactured in recent times for the sole purpose of gaining commercial profit.* These weapons are distinctive in that they are in excellent condition, have a proper Kukri blade and show excellent evidence of a weld on the socket elbow.

After intensive examination, the author has come to the opinion that this bayonet illustrated is not of modern manufacture. Four similar examples are known, all of similar weight but varying slightly in blade dimensions. It is considered likely that these bayonets were manufactured in India, and consist of Native made blades attached to English made sockets. The construction of such pieces could have been to the order of a commander of an Indian volunteer regiment, but this has yet to be proved. The illustrated piece bears the mark JAUREC on the socket. Blade length 16″: overall length 19½″. *Herman A. Maeurer*

45, 46. A Volunteer Baker sword bayonet. This strange piece has a standard pattern Second Pattern Baker bayonet hilt—a cast brass grip with horizontal ribbing; the bayonet bar slot and internal spring are contained within the hilt, and activated by an external stud placed low down on the grip. A cast brass knuckle-bow, quillon and shell guard comprise the crosspiece.

The outstanding feature of this bayonet is the straight broad blade, secured to the hilt by a tang projecting through the pommel and bossed over, which is quite unlike any regular pattern of this bayonet.

The blade is straight and single-edged, a short ricasso can be noted at the juncture with the hilt on the reverse of the blade. No fullering exists anywhere on the blade. The back and true edge of the blade are parallel to within 3″ of the tip, and the blade width (constant throughout) is 2½″.

The scabbard is a black leather, containing wood liners, and is double-stitched on the reverse. Brass fittings cover the throat with a frog stud placed on the face of the locket. The chape is similarly styled, but contoured to the tip of the blade.

No information has yet been located concerning this example: it is, in all probability, a volunteer pattern, *c.* 1820. Blade length 23″: overall length 28″. *R. D. C. Evans*

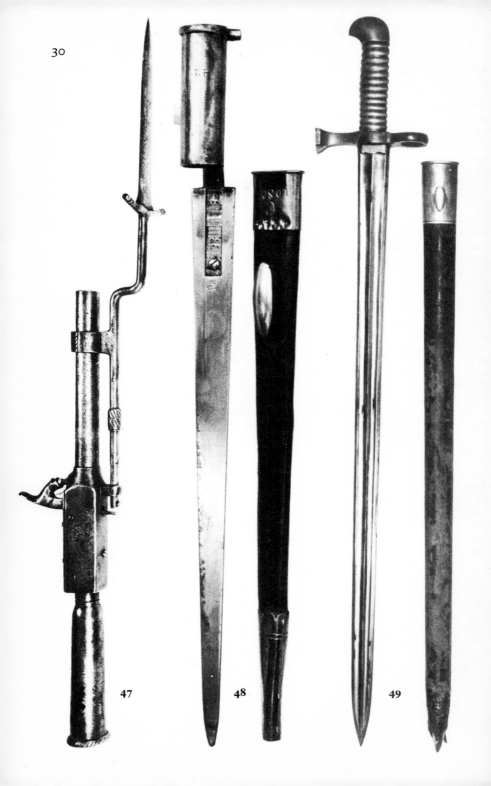

30

47   48   49

47. An interesting combination polearm, pistol and bayonet—perhaps of Belgian make—*c.* 1830. The weapon is primarily a polearm while the bayonet serves the dual purpose of acting as a blade and triggering the pistol. When a thrust was made into an adversary, the bayonet triggers the action and the pistol completes the *coup de grâce. Weller & Dufty*

48. A socket bayonet for the Royal Irish Constabulary, 1840. An interesting feature of this bayonet is the spring clip situated on the face of the blade between the shoulders, broken on the illustrated example. The purpose of this device was to secure the bayonet in the scabbard —not to prevent accidental loss of the bayonet but to make it more difficult to wrench the bayonet from the constable.

The scabbard is black leather with a steel liner and a brass locket and throat. Issue numbers are to be noted on this portion, 1080 on the example illustrated, with the letter 'C' for Constabulary. Suspension was by means of a leather frog attached to an elongated frog stud brazed to the liner and projecting through the leather. The tip of the scabbard terminates in a brass chape. Blade length 12″: overall length 16½″. *S & G Arms*

49. A European Customs bayonet, *c.* 1841. Strictly, this item would be more appropriately called a side-arm, though its design is more akin to that of a bayonet. The hilt is made of brass, horizontally ribbed, but contains no provision for fixture of the item to a rifle, although the crossguard possesses a muzzle ring. The crossguard is made of steel, and the quillon terminates into a broad face which is intended for use as a seal. This was originally used by Customs officers who were passing goods as cleared from duty. As merchandise was examined, it was marked on the side of the container by stamping with the quillon. This mark would give details of

where the goods were examined, and the number of the official who had examined them. The blade is straight, without cutting-edges (it was probably intended for such tasks as prising open crates), and is double fullered on both sides. An interesting manner of assembly occurs with this item in that the blade tang passes through the hilt, and is held in position by means of a threaded tube which screws onto the tang flush with the pommel. The scabbard is wood, with a brown leather covering, and the throat and tip (missing on illustrated item) fittings are made of brass. Blade length 22½″: overall length 27″. *F. J. Stephens*

50. A detail of the quillon on the Customs bayonet, showing the lettering 'CV 3'. The actual dimensions of the item illustrated are: upper part ¾″ wide; lower part ⅜″ wide; overall depth ⅞″. *F. J. Stephens*

51

51. An M1842 French Sabre bayonet. The grooved hilt is a brass casting with a press stud and an external locking spring. The steel crosspiece has a rearward sweeping quillon. The place of origin is usually found engraved along the back edge, together with the date of manufacture. Blade length 22⅝″: overall length 27½″. *Dr. John Kennaugh*

52. A bayonet for the Irish Constabulary Carbine, 1848. It is similar to the Brunswick bayonet pattern of 1847; the blade is the same length, 22″, but this weapon has longer fullers. *S & G Arms*

53. A Swiss bayonet for the Federal rifle *c.* 1850. The blade of this piece is typical of the type manufactured on socket bayonets of this period but, due to the unusual locking system, it cannot be accurately classified as a socket bayonet as no such item exists on the piece. Attachment to the rifle was by means of a dovetailed groove which mated with a channel on the barrel. Originally the piece was blued. Blade length 20″: overall length 24″. *Herman A. Maeurer*

54. A European plug bayonet, *c.* 1850. This sporting bayonet, possibly of Spanish manufacture, is a rather fine example with a turned ivory grip and brass fittings. The blade is decorated with pierced fullering, a practice quite popular with the Spanish smiths of the period. The use of the plug bayonet during the eighteenth and nineteenth centuries was popularised mainly by the hunting fraternity, who liked to adorn themselves with selected blades for dress purposes, which could also be used when engaged in 'sport'. Private dress weapons in the form of bayonets were not greatly popular in England and it seems to have been the Spanish and French who adopted the majority of these weapons. German hunters also wore bayonets as an accoutrement—but a preference for hunting swords made the dress bayonet a minority choice. Swordsmiths in Solingen manufactured sporting plug bayonets for sale to other European markets, but it appears to have been the Spanish who captured the greater part of the trade, as German markings on these weapons appear to be somewhat scarce. *Weller & Dufty*

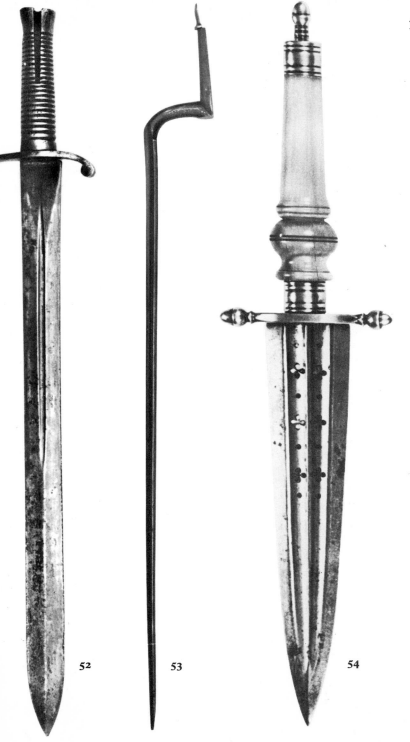

52   53   54

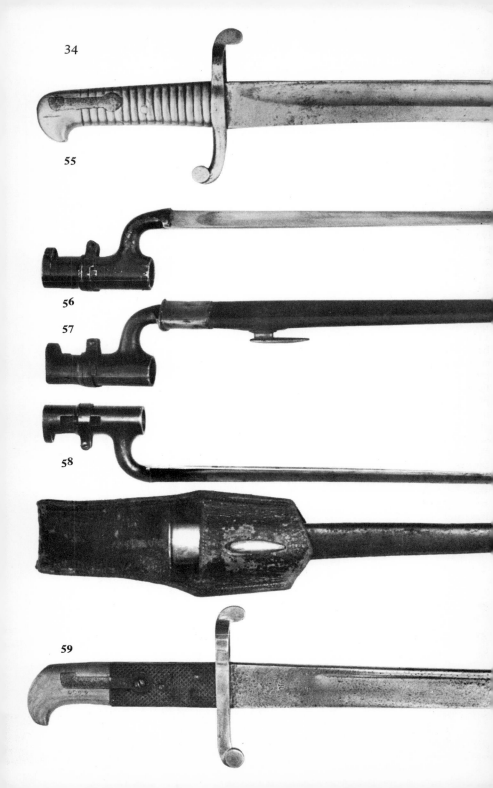

34

55

56

57

58

59

55. A British sabre bayonet, Pattern 1852, for the experimental Artillery Carbine Pattern 1852. Based on the design of the French 1842 sabre bayonet, examples of this bayonet are very rare. The hilt is brass, ribbed and inset with slot and spring. The crossguard is steel with an upswept quillon, and a down-swept muzzle ring quillon. The blade is single-edged, fullered and recurving. The bayonet was manufactured as an experimental piece only and within a few years was replaced by the more common-ly encountered steel hilt and leather grip pattern sabre bayonets. Blade length 22½″: overall length 27¼″. *R. D. C. Evans*

56, 57. The Pattern 1853 Socket bayo-net. Two types of this weapon exist, differing solely in weight: the earlier version weighing 11 oz and the later one 13½ oz. This was the first British socket bayonet with a locking ring to become standard service issue. At least seven companies had contracts for the manu-facture of these items and, although all products conformed to a weight re-quirement, some minor variation can be encountered in blade lengths. The sockets of the bayonets were blued but the blades were left untreated. The blades are triangular in cross section, with fullers on all three faces and the scabbards are made of black leather with brass fittings. In 1871 many of these bayonets were officially bushed for the newly-introduced Marini-Henry rifle. Then in 1876 a bayonet was approved for the Marini-Henry, similar to the Enfield 1853 pattern but having a longer blade

—after this date all 1853/71 Enfield socket bayonets were declared obsolete and withdrawn from service once the new bayonets became available. Blade length 17″: overall length 22½″. *Ken Holdich*

58. A Pattern 1853 socket bayonet. This example shows the frog pattern fitted with the original scabbard. *S & G Arms*

59. The Lancaster sword bayonet, Pat-tern 1855; a most distinctive bayonet pattern with pipe-back blade and spear-point tip, the hilt is brass with slot and spring fixture. The grips are made of black chequered leather secured by four steel rivets. The crossguard bears a quillon and, on the opposite side, a muzzle ring. Because the Lancaster bayonet was a side fitting type, the face edge of the muzzle ring is ground flat to permit sighting. The scabbard is made of black leather, with brass fittings. Blade length 23½″: overall length 28″. *Ken Holdich*

60. A sabre bayonet for the Enfield Short Rifle. The bayonet itself is a standard pattern, but the scabbard has the most unusual feature of being rein-forced with a specially-designed attach-ment on the tip. The purpose of this was probably for attaching an entrenching tool in order that the scabbard could be utilised as a form of spade. The scabbard body is leather, reinforced with steel. Fittings are steel and highly polished. Blade length 22¾″: overall length 28″. *Bernard Marsh*

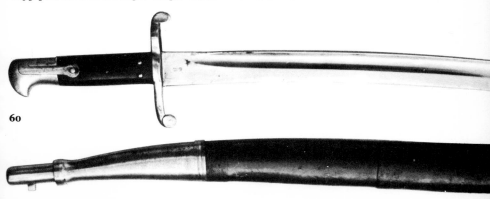

60

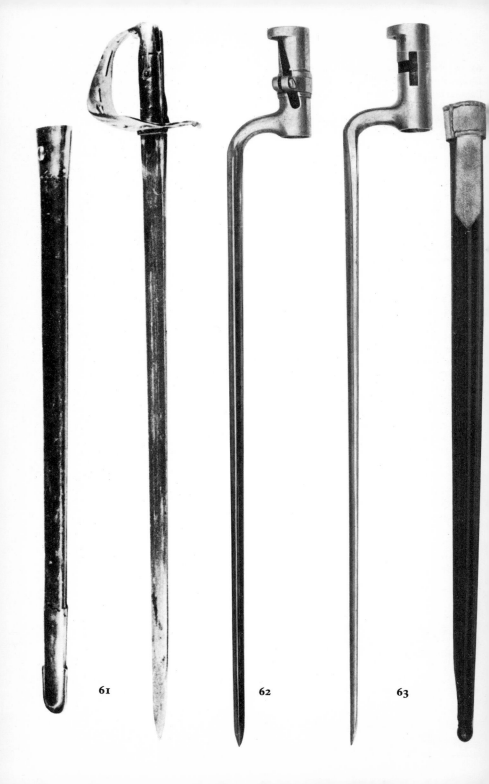

61   62   63

61. A sword bayonet for the Jacob's Double-barrelled Rifle, 1856. These bayonets and the rifle they fitted were designed by General John Jacob, Officer Commanding the Scinde Irregular Horse in India.

Regardless of the efforts made by Jacob on behalf of the rifle of his design, neither it nor the bayonet was ever officially accepted for use as a standard service issue weapon for troops of the Indian Army. However, at least one regiment was equipped with the rifles and bayonets, the 1st Regiment of Jacob's Rifles, and the expense of equipping this unit was borne by Jacob himself. The Jacob's sword bayonet is extremely rare and as a bayonet pattern quite distinctive. The hilt is in the form of a basket, the guard bearing an elaborate scroll design with provision for the double-barrelled muzzle. The grips are made of chequered leather riveted to the blade tang, and a slot and spring mechanism is incorporated in the pommel. The blade is straight and double-edged, with double fullers on each side. The scabbard is leather with brass fittings. A number of variations are encountered in the range of Jacob's bayonets, and it appears that some volunteer regiments adopted the rifle and bayonet for use. Among the manufacturers of the bayonets and rifles are noted John Manton, Swinburn & Son, Robert Garden and Witton & Daw. Blade length 30″. *Weller & Dufty*

62. An Austrian socket bayonet for use with the Lorenz Musket, c. 1856. A distinctive feature on most Austrian socket bayonets is the foresight slot, which curves around the socket, unlike most other types in which this feature is made with 'corners'. The blade is straight and double-edged. During the American Civil War, many of these bayonets and rifles were purchased by the United States Government to supplement the limited supplies available to their troops; they were mainly carried by the New York and Texas Militia Regiments. Blade length 18½″: overall length 22″. *Herman A. Maeurer*

63. An American Socket bayonet for the Maynard Tape Primer musket, Model 1857. The establishment of the United States Armouries did not come about until 1796. Prior to this time the bayonets and muskets used were mainly imported weapons from England and France and, even after the establishment of the Armouries, bayonets were manufactured for use on imported rifles. Where deemed by necessity the importation of bayonets continued well into the second half of the 19th century. On the item illustrated the scabbard is of French manufacture, although the bayonet is American made. It is interesting to note that no locking ring was incorporated in the design of this piece. The bayonet is made of steel, and the scabbard of black leather with a white leather throat. Blade length 18″: overall length 21¼″. *Herman A. Maeurer*

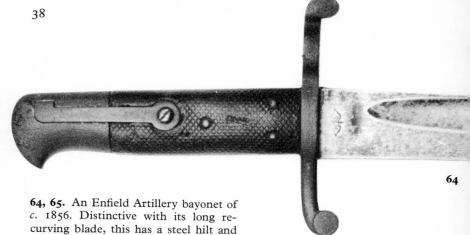

64

64, 65. An Enfield Artillery bayonet of
c. 1856. Distinctive with its long recurving blade, this has a steel hilt and
quillons, with black chequered leather
grips. Manufacture of these pieces was
not restricted to England, for German
firms in the famed industrial steel town
of Solingen also produced them to
contract. The specimen illustrated is of
German manufacture. Distinct differences in blade lengths are to be encountered, though it is probable that the
majority of these variations were the
product of the continental manufacture.
Blade length 22¾″: overall length 28″.
Ken Holdich

66. A Spanish Artillery Carbine bayonet, Model 1858. This is a very distinctive bayonet and the issue scabbard for
this pattern (not illustrated) is black
leather with brass fittings. The hilt is
made of cast brass with a 'flaming bomb'
emblem cast into both faces of the pommel. The grip is horizontally ribbed and
terminates in a steel crossguard which
consists of a single upswept quillon on
one side, and a socket with locking ring
on the other. The whole of the crossguard is blued. The blade is single edged,
with a short false edge at the tip. The

broad ricasso is etched on one side
FABRICA DE TOLEDO and, on the illustrated example, ANNO D 1860 on the
other side. A deep fuller runs the length
of the blade to the false edge on both
sides. Blade length 17½″: overall length
22¾″. *Weller & Dufty*

67. A French-made sabre-bladed socket
bayonet for the Perrin Military Revolv-
ing Rifle, *c.* 1860. A very limited number
of these pieces were supplied to the
Union Forces in the American Civil
War, but the arm was never officially
adopted by either France or the U.S.A.
Blade length 21¼″: overall length 25¾″.
R. D. C. Evans

68. A steel hilted volunteer bayonet
with a Lancaster blade *c.* 1860. The hilt
is of Enfield pattern but bears a barrel
ring of larger dimension, rifle model
unknown. The scabbard is leather with
steel fittings, and the grips are chequered
leather. Blade length 22″: overall length
27¼″. *S & G Arms*

67

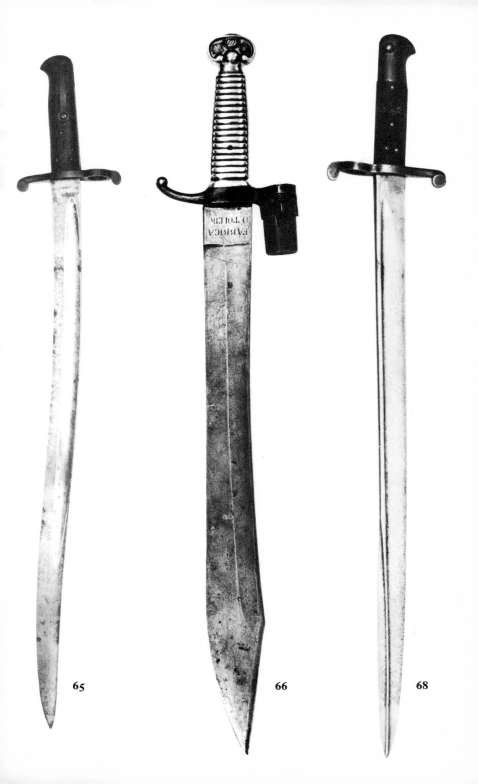

65   66   68

69

70

71

69. The Dahlgren Bowie bayonet for the US Navy Rifle, Model 1861. The bayonet shown in this illustration is a modern reproduction, originals of this pattern are very scarce. However, the bayonet is a facsimile of the original pattern and details of the original type are listed herein. The hilt is brass, with a rifle-slot cut in the backstrap, and containing a spring release with press-stud on the face. The contoured grip is made of walnut and the crossguard of brass, with one upswept quillon and one terminating in the muzzle-ring. The blade is straight and single-edged, with a 5½″ false-edge. The bayonet was designed to fit the American Navy Rifle, Model 1861 and was believed to have been designed by Admiral John Dahlgren, USN. At least four patterns of the Dahlgren Bowie bayonet have been recorded:

M1861; usually dated '1861' on the ricasso, and distinctive in that the grip is secured with three copper pins. *M1861 variation*; this is basically the same as the above, but differs in that the grip is secured by a single copper pin. *M1862 and M1863*; two patterns of similar type usually distinguished by the date. The mark DR appears in script in an oval on the pommel and this lettering is repeated on the ricasso—which is also marked USN (see illustration). *M1864*; these are the same as above, but have the markings DR and GG included as well as the date '1864'. The DR stands for Daniel Reynolds, US Navy Inspector, and the GG for Commander Guert Gansevoort USN. The scabbards for the bayonets are made of black leather with a brass throat and chape. Blade length 12⅛″: overall length 16⅞″. *Herman A. Maeurer*

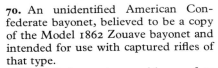

70. An unidentified American Confederate bayonet, believed to be a copy of the Model 1862 Zouave bayonet and intended for use with captured rifles of that type.

The hilt is cast brass with a surface finish in a feathered design. A locking slot and spring are contained in the pommel, and steel crossguard similar in design to the Model 1842 French Sabre bayonet.

Like the French bayonet, the blade is slightly recurved, single-edged and fullered. Blade length 20″. *F. J. Stephens*

71. A sword bayonet for the American Sharps and Hankins rifle, Model 1863. Having a brass hilt, not unlike the French M42 sabre bayonet, this pattern is quite similar to that manufactured for the Sharps rifle. However, in 1863 the company of Christian Sharps associated with that of William C. Hankins and produced a new rifle pattern, to which was added the new pattern bayonet. The crossguard is steel, with a slightly downswept quillon. The blade is single edged, fullered on both sides and slightly recurving. The scabbard, not illustrated, has a leather body with brass fittings. Blade length 20¼″: overall length 25″. *Herman A. Maeurer*

72. An M1866 French sabre bayonet commonly called a 'Chassepôt'. Similar to a preceding design—the M1842—but with a lightened blade and a forward sweeping quillon. Blade length 22½″: overall length 27½″. *Dr. John Kennaugh*

73. An Austrian socket bayonet for use with the Jäger rifle Model 1840/67. All steel in construction, the bayonet fitted to the rifle by means of the socket, cut with a curved foresight slot, and held firmly in position by means of the locking collar. The blade is broad, straight and single-edged, with a double-edged tip. It was used by Jäger Regiments but some Pioneer Regiments were issued with a similar bayonet with a saw back. Blade length 23″: overall length 28″. *Herman A. Maeurer*

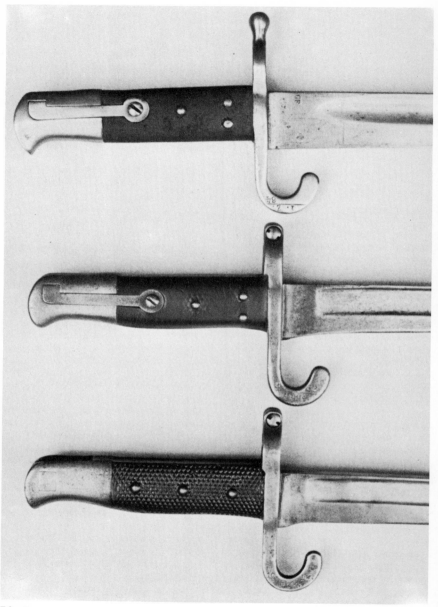

74, 75, 76. Bayonets produced for use with the Austrian Werndl rifle, Model 1867 and its successors. The improvements of the basic pattern is clearly shown on this illustration between the earlier item, on the right, and the later type shown on the left. Refinements in manufacture and advancement in design are quite distinct in the improvement of the grip, contour and chequering, adoption of an interior placed locking spring, and refinement of the crossguard which are evident in the progressive stages of variation shown on the three items above: Top, Model 1873, Blade length 18½″, overall length 23¾″; Centre, Model 1870, with shortened blade (originally 23¾″) length, 18½″, overall length, 23¾″; Bottom, Model 1867, issued to infantry and rifle regiments. Blade length 22¼″, overall length 28″. *R. D. C. Evans*

77. A Danish sabre bayonet of unidentified pattern. Probably manufactured

c. 1870. Full details about this piece have not yet been traced, but it is believed that the bayonet was one of a type specially manufactured for use on rifles which had been converted to the Snider breech loading system. The bayonet was manufactured in Germany, by the firm of Gebrüder Weyersberg, to Danish Government contract. The style of the hilt is most interesting, being strikingly like an Enfield type. Quite possibly the German manufacturer made use of hilt castings, or even modified some spare hilts that had been manufactured for British bayonets. Blade length 22″: overall length 27″. *R. D. C. Evans*

78. Danish Model 1867 sabre bayonet manufactured for use on the Remington Rolling Block rifle M1867. Manufactured in Germany by Gebrüder Weyersberg, Solingen. Blade length 21⅞″: overall length 26¾″. *R. D. C. Evans*

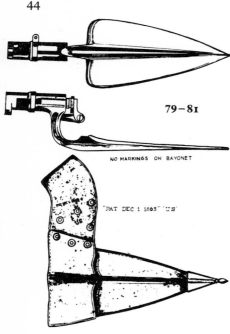

79–81

NO MARKINGS ON BAYONET

"PAT DEC 1 1863" "U S"

79, 80, 81. A Model 1868 United States Trowel bayonet. This socket bayonet design was originally conceived to act both as a bayonet and an entrenching tool. It was designed to fit the U.S. Musket model 1855/70, Cal 0.58″. The scabbard is made of brown leather, with a 'loop' style frog, secured to the scabbard by means of seven copper rivets. Blade length $8\frac{3}{4}$″: blade width $3\frac{15}{16}$″. *Drawing by M. H. Cole*

82. A shortened Martini-Enfield bayonet used for drill purposes. Originally this bayonet was a P56 Enfield sword bayonet, but in 1888 the muzzle ring was rebushed for the Martini-Metford rifle. In 1895 these bayonets became obsolete, most of them were then officially shortened and used for drill purposes, designated the Martini-Enfield bayonet, 1895. Blade length 13″: overall length $18\frac{1}{2}$″. *Ken Holdich*

83. Although not to be regarded as 'true' bayonets, miniature bayonets do offer some interest to collectors. The item illustrated above is particularly interesting, being a complete miniature Martini rifle, with a miniature bayonet capable of being fixed to the barrel. The bayonet is not a complete facsimile of the type fitted to this arm, but, nonetheless, it makes an attractive item and interesting talking piece. Overall length of bayonet $9\frac{1}{2}$″. *Weller & Dufty*

84. A United States Navy bayonet for the Remington rifle, Model 1870. Two similar patterns of this bayonet exist, differing only in the blade style. The blade length and hilt design of both patterns is identical, and both were issued in brass mounted leather scabbards. The illustrated example has a cast brass hilt with the emblem of two crossed Dahlgren naval guns superimposed over an anchor in the pommel. The grip finish simulates fish scales and the crossguard and barrel ring are of brass and part of the hilt casting.

The blade is secured to the hilt by means of the tang passing longitudinally through the grip, but the tang projection does not extend beyond the pommel. This has been so designed that the tang finish is contained within a recess below the pommel head, the upper part of the recess being designed to accommodate the ramrod of the rifle which, when attached, will project forward into the recess. Attachment to the arm is by means of a mortise cut within the back of the grip, and a press stud and spring to lock the bayonet in position. The spring may be observed fitted externally to a recess in the hilt. The blade is single edged, fullered, and slightly recurving. A variation of this pattern has a straight blade of identical length, although both patterns fit the same black leather scabbard. Blade length $20\frac{1}{8}$″: overall length $24\frac{3}{4}$″. *Weller & Dufty*

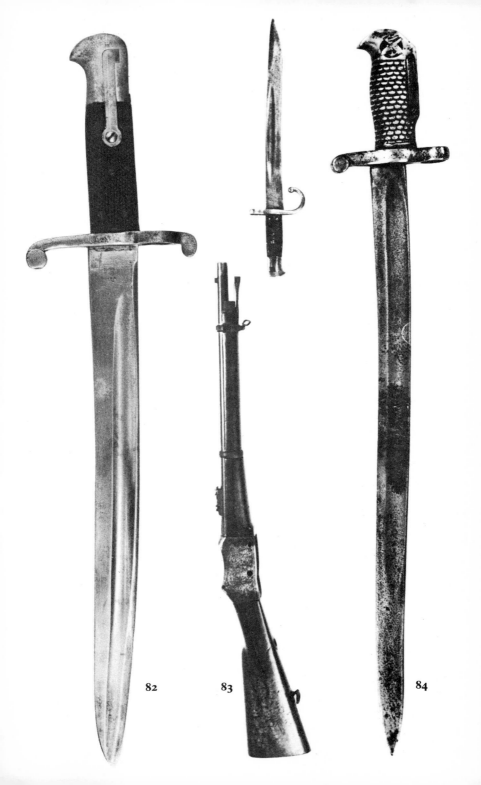

82   83   84

46

85

86

85. The Elcho sword bayonet, Pattern 1870, passed for use in February 1871. This bayonet was designed by Lord Elcho, and was first used in service in the Ashanti War of 1873–74. The bayonet was issued in limited numbers and, it is believed, it was restricted to the 42nd Regiment, the 23rd Regiment and the 2nd Battalion, the Rifle Brigade. It was used with the Snider rifle. The first issue of 1870 was made in .577 calibre, but a second type of 1871 was for the Martini, in .45″ calibre. The service use of the Elcho bayonet was restricted after 1874, but in 1895 the pattern was revived and reissued. On this occasion only .45 calibre was used, and the bayonet was used with the Martini-Henry rifle. The example illustrated has a steel pommel with a slot and spring mechanism cut into it. The grips are made of checkered leather, secured to the tang by four rivets. The crossguard extends into a muzzle ring on the side, and a quillon, slightly upswept on the other. The saw-back blade is most distinctive, swelling to a spear point at the tip. It has been suggested this feature was inspired by the *assagai* spears frequently encountered by the British soldiers when engaged in native wars. The scabbard is black leather with steel fittings; the throat of the scabbard having a vertical D-shaped frog bar brazed to it, through which the leather frog was buckled. Some examples of the bayonet have brass scabbard fittings, a feature which appears to be restricted to a German arms firm who manufactured the bayonet. Blade length $19\frac{1}{2}″$: overall length $25\frac{1}{4}″$. *J. Anthony Carter*

86. A German Mauser bayonet, Model 1871. The illustrated weapon is a special 'dress', or walking out, bayonet. It differs from the standard issue in that the blade is finely etched.

The use of 'dress' bayonets among military personnel was very popular among ranks who were not entitled to wear swords. Special 'dress' bayonets were permitted to be worn, but purchase of the weapons was the liability of owner. Many variations may be encountered in the privately purchased pieces, varying from dress blades fitted to standard type hilts, to completely distinctive patterns with no provisions for attachment to a rifle.

Blade types varied from plain nickel-plated blades to finely etched patterns with special dedications. The use of dedications covered a wide range, often listing regimental numbers and sometimes the owner's name. Frequently it was practice for a soldier's family to buy a special 'dress' bayonet to mark the commencement of a military career, or the termination of years of service. In the cases where the individual or his family considered the cost of a private dedication too great, a standard dedication could be purchased at less cost than that required for the making of a private template. Most popular among the standard dedications were the words: ZUR ERINNERUNG AN MEINE DIENSTZEIT (In memory of my military service), a favourite alternative to this was an etched blade without dedication—just an ornation of floral scroll work. Blade length $18\frac{1}{2}″$: overall length $23\frac{1}{2}″$. *Weller & Dufty*

87. A British Pattern 1859 Cutlass bayonet, converted in 1871 for the Martini-Henry rifle. The muzzle-ring diameter has been reduced by an eccentric bushing. The grips are made of compressed chequered leather, secured by four rivets. A steel basket protects the hand when the bayonet is used as a cutlass. Blade length 26¾″: overall length 32¼″. *R. D. C. Evans*

88. An Imperial German 'dress' bayonet, of the Mauser 1871 Model. Although the hilt of this example is fitted with a locking spring, no mortise is cut in the pommel and hence it cannot be fitted to a rifle. It was worn purely for 'undress' and walking-out purposes. The hilt is brass, diagonally grooved for grip, with a steel crosspiece in the form of up-swept and down-swept quillons, the latter part containing a muzzle ring. The blade is lightly etched with a floral design. The scabbard is made of black leather, with brass fittings; a black leather frog is attached to the scabbard and tied round the body of the frog is a troddel made of white cloth with blue body. The purpose of the troddel is to show the company colours of the wearer although not giving a precise identification of the regiment. Blade length 19⅛″: overall length 23½″. *R. D. C. Evans*

89. A Prussian pionierfaschinenmesser M1871. The brass hilt has a steel crosspiece and steel quillons in the form of a shallow S. The wide, heavy blade is quite distinctive with its wide fuller and serrated back edge. The black leather scabbard has brass fittings. Blade length 18¾″: overall length 23⅞″. *J. Anthony Carter*

90. Imperial German 'dress' bayonet, with etched blade, in the style of the *Jäger Hirschfänger* bayonet M1871.

Although functional as a bayonet, it was only used for walking out and parade purposes. The hilt is polished steel, with rifle slot and spring cut in the pommel. The grips are made of chequered leather, riveted to the hilt by five rivets. The cross piece is steel, having the muzzle ring on one side, and terminating into an up-swept quillon. The ricasso of the blade clearly shows the trade mark of Weyersberg, Kirschbaum & Company, Solingen Armourers, and the pattern of trade mark is one that was not in use prior to 1883, thus giving a clear indication of the earliest possible date of manufacture. The blade is straight, single-edged and fullered on both sides. The tip of the blade swells to spear point. Both sides of the blade are finely etched with a typical hunting scene embellishment, showing a hunter, deer and floral design. Blade length 19⅛″: overall length 23¼″. *R. D. C. Evans*

91, 92. Imperial German sword bayonets, for the 1871 Mauser rifle, also used with the model 1884 Mauser rifle. Brass hilts, steel crossguards. The model on left is the standard infantry version, the saw-back bladed pattern on right was issued to infantry NCOs. Proportions of both pieces are identical. Blade length 18⅜″: overall length 23½″. *R. D. C. Evans*

87

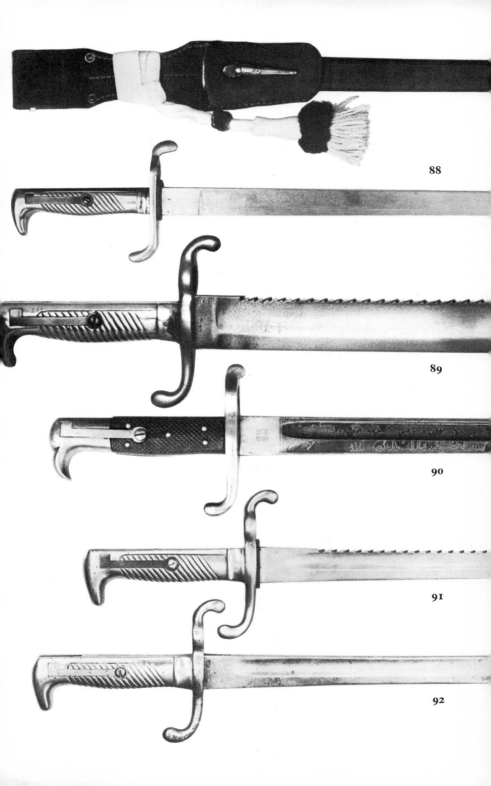

88

89

90

91

92

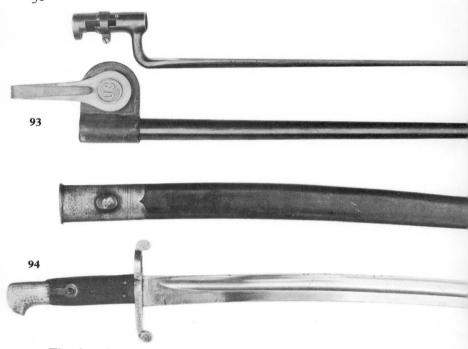

93. The American socket bayonet for the Springfield .45/70 rifle, model 1873.

The blade of the bayonet is triangular, and the whole of the socket and blade is blued. The bayonet is secured to the rifle by means of a locking collar and screw.

The scabbard is made of blued steel, and the frog stitched to the throat and made of black leather. Belt suspension is by means of a brass belt-hook, with the marking 'US' on the lower section. Blade length 18″: overall length 21¼″.
Herman A. Maeurer

94. An Enfield Artillery bayonet, Pattern 1853, modified model. This example has a re-bushed muzzle ring, and the pommel is stamped M.D.S.R.A.M.C.—denoting that the bayonet has been issued to the Royal Army Medical Corps, established in 1873. In all other respects the bayonet is identical to the model 1853 pattern.
Ken Holdich

95, 96, 97, 98. A Model 1873 trowel bayonet made for the Springfield rifle. The production of these bayonets is believed to have been limited to 10,000 and it was not regarded as a completely successful design. Several distinctive features are incorporated in this extremely novel design of bayonet, such as the two-piece socket fitting. This is constructed with an inner key-way and, when the bayonet is attached to the rifle, the rear end of the socket can be twisted 90 degrees to lock it in position. The blade bears a strong resemblance to a mason's trowel—hence the name. Blade length 11″: overall length 14½″.
R. D. C. Evans

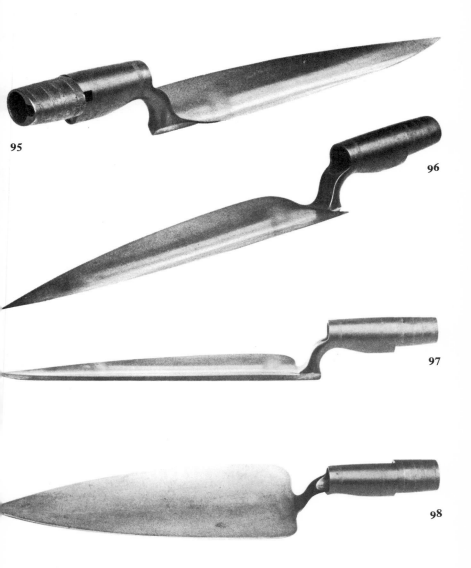

95

96

97

98

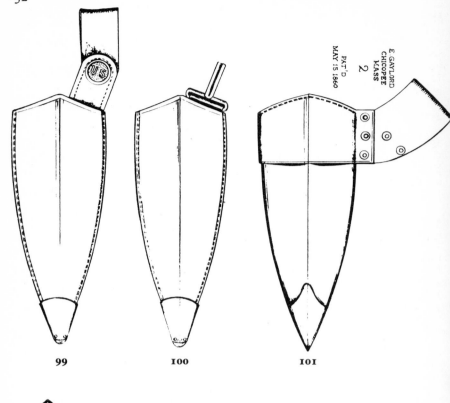

99   100   101

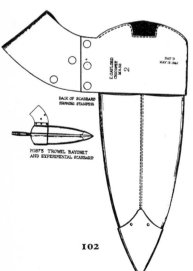

102

99, 100, 101. Three scabbard patterns designed for the Model 1873 Trowel bayonet. All three are made of black leather with brass fittings. *Drawing by M. H. Cole*

102. A variation pattern of scabbard for the Model 1873 Trowel bayonet. This pattern of scabbard is similar to the Model 1869 scabbard (patented May 15, 1960) and is believed to be an experimental pattern. The belt loop is held in position by five copper rivets and the scabbard is made of black leather, with brass fittings. *Drawing by M. H. Cole*

103. A French Gras bayonet, M1874. The weapon has a brass pommel with wooden grips and a long straight, T section blade. The steel crosspiece has a pronounced quillon. During World War I, quantities of Gras bayonets were modified by the Germans to fit their own rifles. Blade length 20½″: overall length 25⅜″. *Dr. John Kennaugh*

104. The engraving on the back of the Gras blade; MRE D'ARMES DE ST. ETIENNE 8BRE 1879 for 'Manufactured at St. Etienne Arsenal, August 1879'. *F. J. Stephens*

105. French Model 1874 *Enfants de Troupe* bayonet, the miniature cadet version of the 1874 Gras bayonet. The miniature weapon is extremely rare, and two distinct variations of the miniature are known to have been produced. Blade length 15¼″: overall length 18¾″. *R. D. C. Evans*

103 **104**

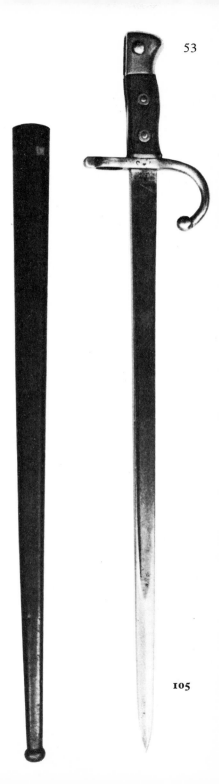

105

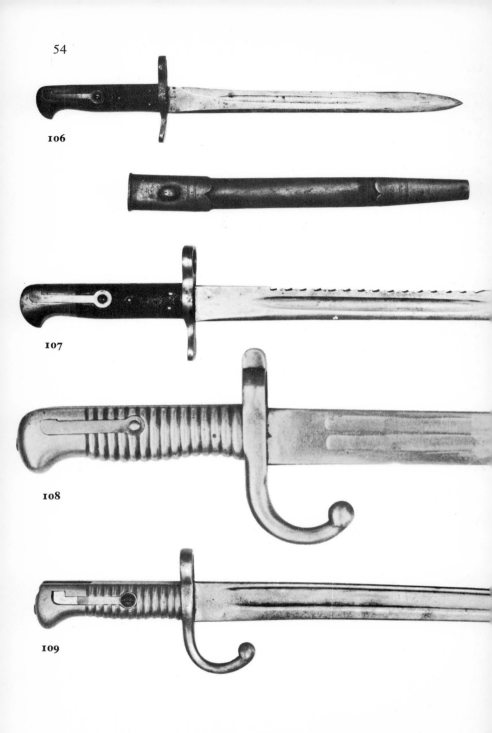

54

106

107

108

109

106. An Artillery sword bayonet, 1875, converted to trench dagger. This conversion may possibly be a factory machined alteration, as it is very effectively executed. The blade has had the saw-back removed and the length shortened to about 12": the scabbard has also been modified to match this piece. In 1903 all the 1875 Artillery bayonets which were in use had the saw-back removed. With the above example it is felt that these were further modified during the First World War, to be used as trench daggers. *S & G Arms*

107. A Martini-Henry sword bayonet, adopted for use by the Royal Artillery in 1875. (Some specimens made for the Snider rifle are encountered, but in the main the Martini-Henry predominates.) The hilt is steel, with black chequered leather grips and the blade is straight, single-edged with a saw-back on the back edge. The scabbard is leather, with steel fittings and an elongated frog stud on the topmount. In 1879 reports were made that the blade length was considered too short, so a new pattern was produced with 25¾" blade. Blade length 18": overall length 25". *Ken Holdich*

108. An unidentified bayonet, possibly of Belgian manufacture, and sold as an export item to such varied countries as Argentine, Venezuela, Belgian Congo etc. The piece probably dates from *c.* 1880. At least three variations of this bayonet exist, distinguished by the fullers of the blade: some having three fullers, as illustrated, some with only one fuller and other examples being without any fuller. The style of the bayonet is that of the 1866 French Chassepôt, though the blade formation differs considerably. The hilt is brass, with slot and spring device, and the crossguard steel. The scabbard is made of steel and was originally blued. All examples studied have revealed that the scabbard is about 4" longer than the blade. No marks of origin, date, issue or type appear anywhere on the bayonet or scabbard. Blade length 19": overall length 24". *R. D. C. Evans*

109. A Belgian Comblain rifle sword bayonet for cadets, Model 1880. Similar in design to the M1868, this bayonet is smaller in overall dimensions. The hilt is brass, with horizontal grip ribbing, inset with press stud and cut with a rifle slot. There is a steel crossguard with a complete muzzle ring and a downswept hook quillon. The blade is slightly recurving, single-edged, and fullered. The tip of the blade is missing, and the rounding of the point appears to have been professionally accomplished, quite possibly as a safety feature to reduce accidents whilst cadets were using the bayonet for training purposes. The scabbard, not illustrated, is leather with brass fittings. Blade length 13¼": overall length 16¾". *Herman A. Maeurer*

56

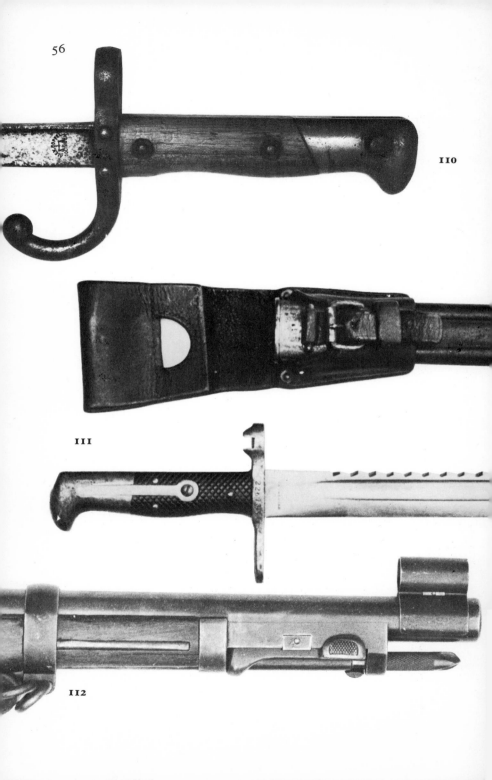

110

111

112

110. A bayonet for the French Kropatschek Naval Rifle, M1878. This is very similar to the M1874 Gras bayonet, but the back of the hilt is entirely flat. The blade, of T section, is $21\frac{1}{2}''$ long. The pommel is brass, the crosspiece of steel and the grips of wood; the markings on the blade show the bayonet to have been made in Germany by the Solingen firm of Alexander Coppel. The bayonet's scabbard is of black painted steel—almost identical to that of the Gras. Blade length $21\frac{1}{2}''$: overall length $27''$. *F. J. Stephens*

111. A Swiss Model 1881 saw-back bayonet for the Vetterli Rifle Model 1881. This type was issued to pioneer troops.

The hilt is steel, with slot and spring fixture, and the grips are made of black chequered leather, secured by three rivets. The blade is straight, single-edged, and fullered on both sides, with saw-teeth cut into the back of the blade. The scabbard is made of leather with steel fittings and was carried by means of a black leather frog attached to the scabbard by means of a buckle. Blade length $18\frac{5}{8}''$: overall length $23\frac{3}{8}''$. *F. J. Stephens*

112, 113. The ramrod bayonet for the Springfield Rifle, Model 1884. This served no function as a ramrod, as the rifle was of breech-loading type. The name 'ramrod bayonet' was popularly bestowed as the bayonet was fitted to the rifle in the same place and manner as the ramrod used on earlier arms. An integral part of the weapon, no scabbard was issued with this piece for, when not in use, it was retracted and stored in the stock below the barrel. A spring clip with press stud secures the rod in either retracted or extended position. Plate 112 shows the bayonet in the retained position, and 113 shows the bayonet withdrawn. Extended length of the bayonet $35\frac{1}{2}''$. *Herman A. Maeurer.*

113

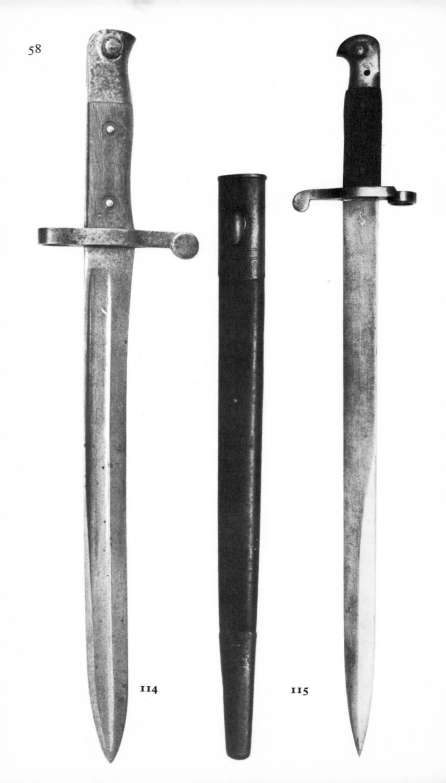

114   115

114. A Portuguese Guedes Rifle bayonet, Model 1885. Manufactured in Austria, at Steyr, this bayonet was originally a sword bayonet with an 18½″ blade. The hilt is steel, with twin slab wood grips secured by two countersunk bolts. The blade is slightly recurved and fullered right to the tip, and single-edged. The back of the blade is marked *Steyr 1885*.

On the original full length examples a small finial was attached to the muzzle ring, but this feature was removed when the modification of the blade was done. *F. J. Stephens*

115. Martini-Henry sword bayonet, pattern 1886. The hilt of this piece is steel, cut with a mortise and locking spring in the pommel. The grips are leather, secured by two countersunk bolts. The crossguard is steel, and bears a stepped down barrel ring. The blade of this weapon is most distinctive, in that it is straight, single edged and unfullered. Unlike most Martini-Henry blades which are yataghan types with fullering. A false-edge extends for 8″ from the tip of the blade. The scabbard is black leather, with steel fittings, a frog stud being affixed to the face of the locket. Suspension was by means of a black leather frog. Blade length 18½″: overall length 25½″. *S & G Arms*

116, 117. A M1886 bayonet for the French Lebel rifle of the same year. It has a slim cruciform blade of 20⅝″, and the locking mechanism appears just behind the crosspiece. The hilts may be of steel or bronze and this particular weapon has a quillon. The French authorities ordered removal of the latter feature in 1915 although some bayonets escaped conversion. The second photograph shows a modified bayonet. Blade length 20⅝″: overall length 25⅛″. *Dr. John Kennaugh*

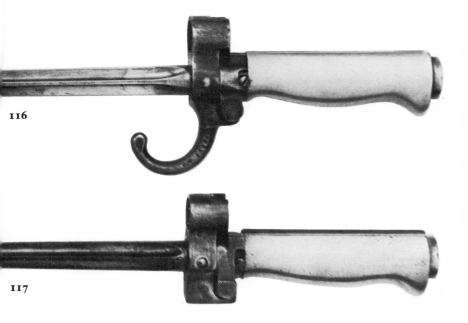

116

117

118

119

118. An Austrian Model 1886 knife bayonet for the Mannlicher rifle, Model 1886. The hilt is steel, with a single quillon comprising of a muzzle ring of 17.5 mm diameter. The grips are twin wood slabs, riveted to the tang.

119. Model 1888 Mannlicher rifle knife bayonet. Almost identical to the left hand item, except that the muzzle ring is 16.5mm in diameter; both bayonets have straight single-edged blades, fullered on both sides.

The ricassos of the blades are marked: on the left Œ/WG—denoting Austrian manufacture; on the right FG/GY—denoting Hungarian manufacture. (At that time Hungary was part of the Austro-Hungarian Empire.) Blade lengths 9¾″: overall length 14¾″. *R. D. C. Evans*

120. A Turkish Mauser bayonet, for the Model 1887 rifle. There is a steel pommel and crosspiece with a down-swept quillon. The wood grips secured by two screws. The blade is straight, single edged and fullered; although the

blade usually bears Turkish markings, translation will show the blade manufacturer to be a German firm. Sometimes variations produced at the turn of the century will have distinctly German style blades, after the 1898 quill-back pattern. The scabbard is leather with steel fittings. Blade length 20¾″: overall length 25¾″. *Tom Greenaway*

121. A Swiss Model 1889 needle bayonet, for the Schmidt-Rubin rifle, Model 1889. An extremely rare pattern of bayonet, manufactured in a unique manner. The blade (cruciform in cross section) is utilized as a blade and hilt combined. Brazed to the end of the blade is a pommel, cut with slot and inset with press stud and spring. The blade is tapered, and so designed that, when the crosspiece is fitted, by being pushed up along the blade it lodges in a position exactly right for fixture to the barrel. The crosspiece is then further secured by brazing and the whole of the bayonet is blued. The pattern is quite rare and was not retained for long. *S & G Arms*

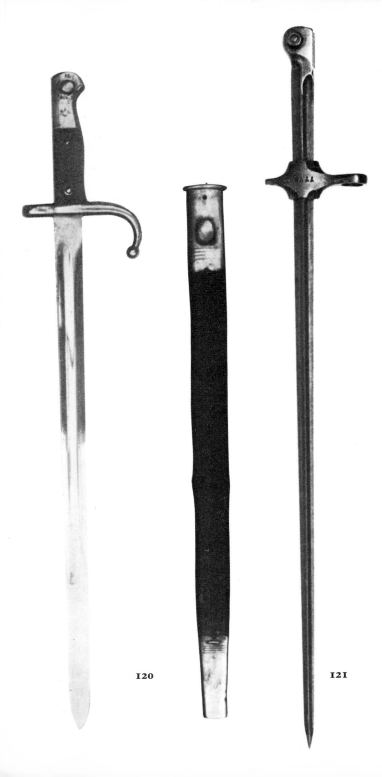

120   121

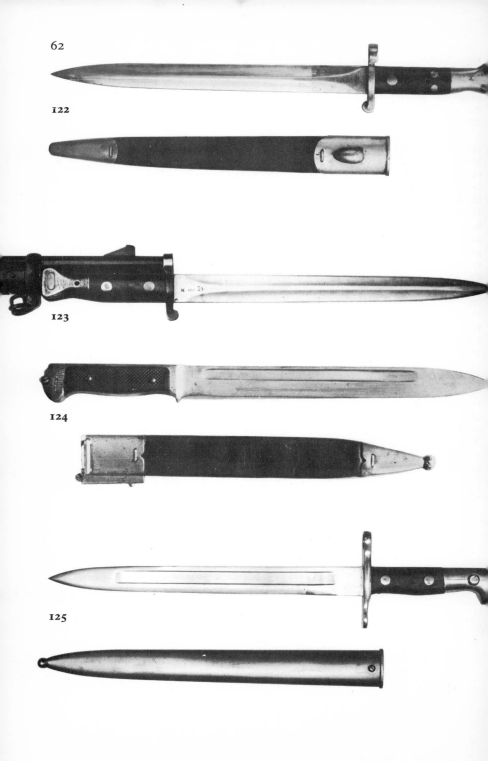

62

122

123

124

125

122. A Pattern 1888 Lee-Metford bayonet (Mk. I.). This bayonet, although termed Pattern 1888, was not approved until June 1889: it was produced after the introduction of the Lee-Metford rifle in 1888.

The metal portions of the hilt were originally browned and three brass rivets held the wood grips in position. An oiling hole was placed in between the two upper rivets. Shortly after introduction the bayonet was replaced by the Mk II bayonet, which differed in that it had only two rivets securing the grips, and the oiling hole was situated in the grip just above the upper rivet. On the example illustrated it will be seen that the pommel is marked with two broad arrows placed point-to-point. This indicates that the bayonet has been declared obsolete and probably sold as an export piece. The scabbard is leather with steel fittings. Blade length 12″: overall length 16¾″. *S & G Arms*

123. A bayonet for the Lee-Enfield rifle of 1895; the bayonet was introduced in the same year and is very similar to that of the Lee-Metford except that it has the oil drainage hole situated in the pommel. The illustrated example is the Pattern 1888 Mk. II, Lee-Enfield and is shown fixed to the rifle. The dimensions of the bayonet are the same as those for the Lee-Metford, the grips are wood and secured by two brass rivets. The blade is straight, double-edged with a rib running the length of the blade and swelling into a ricasso near the hilt. All metal portions of the hilt were originally brown. Blade length 12″: overall length 16¾″. *S & G Arms*

124. A bayonet for the Danish Krag-Jørgensen rifle M1889. The pommel, blade and tang are manufactured from a single piece of steel. The scabbard is leather with steel fittings and the locket contains a locking spring for securing the bayonet in the scabbard. Manufactured in Germany. Blade length 9″: overall length 13¼″. *F. J. Stephens*

125. A short pattern Swiss bayonet for the Schmidt-Rubin rifle of 1889. It has a polished steel pommel and crosspiece, and wooden grips secured by two large steel rivets. The blade is straight, single-edged and fullered: the scabbard is blued steel. Blade length 11½″: overall length 16½″. *J. Anthony Carter*

126. An unidentified pattern of sword bayonet, capable of fitting the Martini Henry rifle. It is thought that this piece may have been a Constabulary issue. Note the three holes in the guard for sighting, barrel and ramrod. Blade length 23½″: overall length 28¾″. *R. D. C. Evans*

126

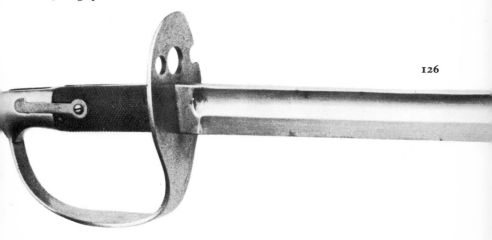

64

127

128

129

127. An Argentine Mauser bayonet, M1891. The pommel and crosspiece are steel, but the grips are of ribbed brass. The blade is straight, single-edged and fullered: the scabbard is steel. Blade length 15¾″: overall length 20½″. *J. Anthony Carter*

128. The Italian Carcano bayonet, Model 1891, special dress pattern.

The principal difference between this bayonet and the standard service issue is that it contains no rifle attachment slot and its purpose was solely for dress wear and walking out. Structurally it is the same as the standard issue, the hilt fittings differ in that it is finely polished, and no mortise or press locking stud is incorporated, though a barrel ring is included. The blade is straight, single-edged and fullered, unlike many service issue blades it is highly polished. The scabbard is standard issue, black leather body with brass fittings, and on the example illustrated the original belt frog is shown attached. Blade length 11¾″: overall length 16¼″. *R. D. C. Evans*

129. Italian folding bayonet fitted to a Carcano carbine Model 1891. This bayonet was designed to be permanently fixed to the rifle and, when not in use, the bayonet was retained with the blade folded back along the barrel. It is secured to the muzzle by an elongated collar screwed into position and the stock of the collar is fitted with a cut-out through which the bayonet folds when moved to—or from—the 'fixed' position. When 'fixed', it locks into position by means of a spring and can only be returned when the spring stud is depressed. The whole of the bayonet is blued, and the blade is 'T' shape in cross-section. Blade length 13¼″: overall length 15″. *Herman A. Maeurer*

130. Russian-made Mosin-Nagant bayonet, Model 1891, but modified with shortened blade and issued to Turkey. This socket bayonet originally had an 18″ blade, cruciform in cross section, but has been shortened to 12″. The tip is a screwdriver pattern and was designed for the purpose of acting as a stripping tool for the rifle. This bayonet pattern has an interesting feature in that the blade is manufactured separately to the socket and shoulder, and was fitted on completion by riveting. Turkey has through the years used various patterns of rifle, purchased as surplus items from various countries, and frequently has purchased bayonets along with the rifles. In some cases bayonets were specially made for the Turks to comply with their own specifications. With the purchase of a large quantity of Mosin-Nagant rifles and accompanying bayonets, the only modification enforced by the Turks was a shortening of the blades. Most of this was done by the Russian authorities selling the arms. In some cases the bayonets were manufactured with short blades for export purposes and, in many cases, Russian armoury markings can be found on these bayonets, though Turkish markings are by no means uncommon. Blade length 12″: overall length 15″. *Ken Holdich*

131. A bayonet for the French M1892 Mousqueton (Berthier). This weapon has black composition grips, a steel pommel and crosspiece and a downswept quillon. The blade is single-edged and fullered with securing recesses into which mate the blade springs contained in the scabbard. Blade length 15¾″: overall length 20¼″. *F. J. Stephens*

130

131

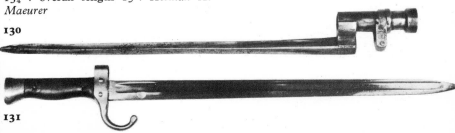

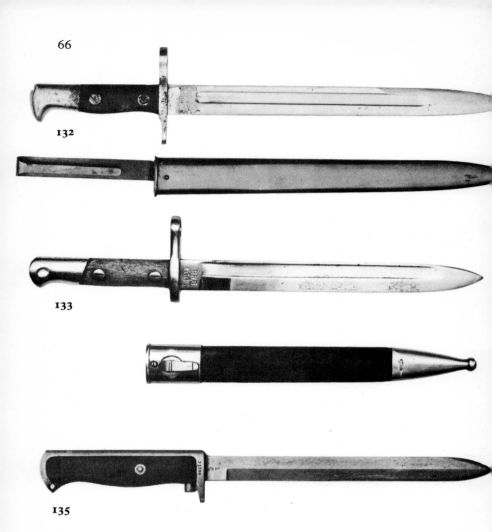

132

133

135

132. The knife bayonet for the United States Krag-Jørgensen rifle Model 1892; the design was based on the Swiss Schmidt-Rubin bayonet of 1889. The hilt of the illustrated pattern is steel, with twin slab wood grips secured by two countersunk screws. The blade is straight, single-edged, and fullered. The ricasso of the blade stamped US and 1892. (The bayonet was manufactured in the United States from 1892 to 1898.) The scabbard is steel with a blued finish, and has a belt-frog loop riveted to the back of the throat. This is made of steel in the form of a hook. Blade length 11½": overall length 16". *Herman A. Maeurer*

133. Bayonet for the Spanish Mauser rifle, model 1893, manufactured in Toledo. The Toledo marking is frequently encountered on the ricasso, though not on all examples. The hilt is polished steel, with a slot and spring mechanism set in the pommel. The grips are twin wooden slabs, secured by means of two countersunk bolts and nuts. The blade is straight, single-edged and fullered on both sides. The scabbard is made of soft black leather, stitched at the back, and with two polished steel fittings stapled in position. Blade length 10″: overall length 15″. *F. J. Stephens*

134. Spanish Mauser bayonet, long type, for the model 1893 Spanish Mauser rifle. Manufactured in Toledo, Spain, most examples of this bayonet originally had the Toledo arsenal marking on the ricasso, but have been ground off before the bayonets were released for sale after becoming obsolete. The hilt is polished steel, with slot and spring inset in the pommel. Twin slab wood grips, finely chequered, are held in place by two countersunk bolts. The blade is straight and single-edged, with fullering on both sides of the blade.

The body of the scabbard is made of soft black leather with polished steel fittings. An elongated frog stud is set on the face of the upper fitting. Blade length 15″: overall length 20″. *F. J. Stephens*

135. A Norwegian Knife bayonet, Model 1894, designed for issue with the M94 Krag-Jørgensen rifle. The bayonet illustrated is marked on the ricasso Œ over WG, showing that the bayonet was manufactured for the Norwegians at Steyr in Austria. The grips are made of wood and secured by a single nut and bolt. Attachment to the rifle is by means of a slot and a locking spring, activated by the press stud situated on the underside of the grip just behind the quillon. This method of locking serves a dual purpose, as an additional clip projects from the locking spring and is used to secure the bayonet in the scabbard. The scabbard (not illustrated) is steel. The blade is single edged, unfullered, but terminates in a double-edged point. *S & G Arms*

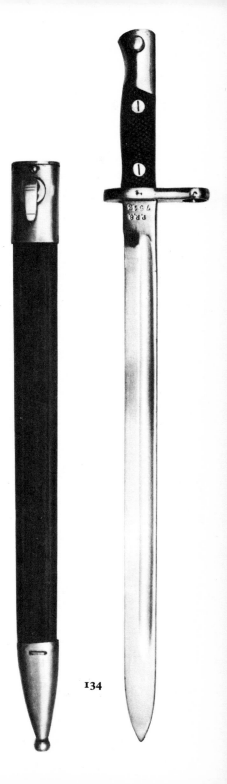

134

68

136   137   138

136. A Norwegian knife bayonet M1894 for the Krag-Jørgensen 6.5mm rifle, and also used on the Krag-Jørgensen M1912 carbine and M1925 Sharpshooter's rifle. This pattern of bayonet was in regular service from its introduction in 1894 through to the end of World War Two. The hilt is steel, cast in one piece and fitted with twin slab contoured wood grips secured to the hilt by one countersunk screw-bolt. A mortise is situated on the back of the hilt, and fitment to the rifle effected by an interior clip and spring activated by the exterior stud placed on the rear face of the hilt. The short quillon serves as a locking device to retain the bayonet in the scabbard, for which purpose a spring clip is situated at the throat. The scabbard is steel, and the blade single-edged and fullered.

During World War II the bayonet was issued to German troops serving in Norway who were equipped with Krag-Jørgensen arms, to Norwegian nationals serving in the German Army, and also to serving members of the Norwegian SS. Blade length 14½″: overall length 19″. *Herman A. Maeurer*

137, 138. A sword bayonet manufactured by the Winchester Repeating Arms Co. for use with the 1895 Military Model Winchester rifle. The hilt is steel, the pommel being cut with rifle slot. The release press-stud is situated on the exterior face of pommel. Twin slab wood grips are fixed to the tang by means of two countersunk bolts and the crossguard is steel with no quillon. The blade is straight, single-edged and fullered. Most of these pieces were sold to the Tsarist Russian Government to supplement the arms available during World War I. Blade length 16″: overall length 21″. *R. D. C. Evans*

139, 140, 141. The Austrian Mannlicher rifle bayonet, Model 1895. This (139) is the standard infantry version and it should be noted that the blade of the bayonet has the cutting edge on the same side as the muzzle ring—a feature introduced in 1895 and intended for all bayonets of this pattern. An Austrian Mannlicher rifle bayonet, Model 1895, NCO's model (140). This is very similar to the infantry version, but differs in that it has a hook quillon and swivel ring on the pommel. The purpose of these was for the attachment of a *portepee*, looped through the swivel and tied round the quillon. A variation of the NCO's 1895 knife bayonet (141), but having the cutting edge of the blade reversed, i.e. being away from the muzzle ring. This variation is not common. All these bayonets were issued in steel scabbards, and the NCO dress versions were usually chrome plated. Blade lengths 9¾″: overall lengths 14½″. *R. D. C. Evans*

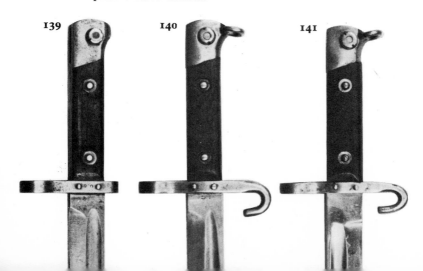

139   140   141

70

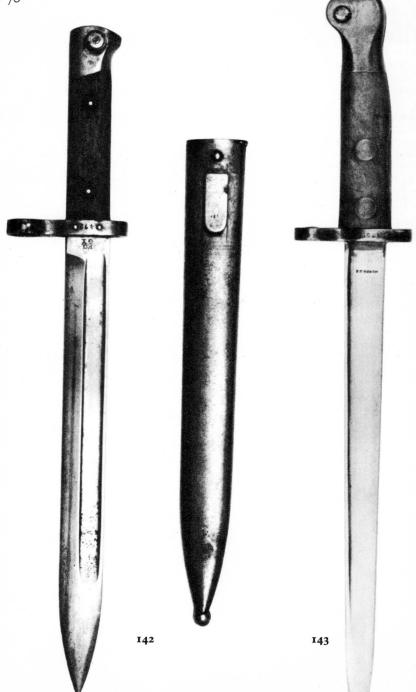

142   143

144

145

142. A bayonet for the Mannlicher Model 1895 rifle, used by the forces of Austria-Hungary before World War I and by various nations thereafter, including Czechoslovakia and Bulgaria. Identical to the Austrian bayonets made by Waffenfabrik Steyr, this weapon was made in Hungary and bears the marking FG over GY on the ricasso. The scabbard is steel with an angular frogstud. Blade length 9¾″: overall length 14″. *Collectors' Arms Antiques Ltd*

143. A Dutch Mannlicher bayonet for the 1895 Mannlicher rifle. The hilt is a copy of the style used on the 1888 British Lee-Metford bayonet and the blade, which is marked HEMBRUG, is T-shaped in cross-section. Blade length 9⅞″: overall length 14⅝″. *R. D. C. Evans*

144. A Dutch cavalry bayonet for use with the M1895 Carbine. The pommel and quillon are made from steel, the blade being straight and double-edged. The wooden grips are secured by two brass rivets passing through the tang, and the brown leather scabbard has a permanently attached belt frog. This specimen bears the manufacturing marks of the Steyr factory in Austria (Œ over WG), but the majority of these bayonets were made at Hembrug Arsenal. *Ken Holdich*

145. A Japanese conversion of a Dutch Model 1895 Cavalry bayonet. Possibly these pieces were captured by the Japanese in the Dutch East Indies during World War II and modified by them for use on the Type 99 Arisaka rifle (Model 1939). With the exception of the modified hilt, the bayonet and scabbard is the same as the original weapon when it was issued by the Dutch. Blade length 10″: overall length 14⅝″. *R. D. Evans*

146

147

148

146. The Swedish bayonet, Model 1896. Made for the Swedish Mauser rifle M1896, this bayonet has a unique style of locking catch: a spring button situated at the top of the all steel hilt (chequered finish) engages on a circular boss on the fore-end of the rifle. Blade length 8¼″: overall length 13⅛″. *R. D. C Evans*

147, 148. Two Japanese bayonets for the Arisaka Type 30 rifle (1897). The introduction of this rifle was brought about by a need to produce a weapon that had less recoil than the 8mm Murata rifle then in current use. The Arisaka rifle was designed by Colonel Nariake Arisaka, chief superintendent of the Tokyo arsenal, in a calibre of 6.5mm. The bayonet designed for the rifle is the Type 30 bayonet with single edged blade and a hilt of slot and spring locking pattern. The pommel, crosspiece and blade are made of steel and were originally blued. Two wood grips cover the hilt and are secured through the tang by means of two countersunk bolts. The upper surface of the crosspiece terminates in a muzzle ring and the lower in a downswept quillon. The blade is single-edged, fullered on both sides and usually bears the manufacturer's mark on the ricasso. The scabbards are made of blued steel and are usually suspended by means of a leather frog buckled through the loop on the scabbard throat. In 1939 a new bayonet was produced, identical to the Type 30 although it was made to fit the newly introduced Type 99 7.7mm Arisaka rifle. Although the quality of the Arisaka bayonet was comparable to European-made pieces, vastly inferior products appeared as a result of the effects on industry during World War II. The downswept quillon was soon replaced by a straight crosspiece and crude hilt patterns lacking in finish were also quite commonplace. Blades too were poorly produced, frequently being un-tempered, and in many cases having the cutting edge extending only on the lower half of the blade. Scabbards were also affected by the economy measures of the war effort and from about 1943 onwards the steel scabbard with leather frog was replaced by a frog and scabbard moulded in one piece out of rubberized canvas. When it became necessary to economise on this, the final product was manufactured out of two pieces of wood, held together with string, and reinforced at the throat and tip by metal bands. Blade length 15⅝″: overall length 20″. *Ken Holdich*

149, 150. M1898 Mauser bayonets manufactured for the Gew. 98. This bayonet is most distinctive with its long quill-backed blade swelling to a spear point at the tip. The hilt is steel, with twin slab wood grips, grooved and secured by two countersunk bolts. It is known that the earlier version of this bayonet had been manufactured in limited quantity and were distinguished by heavy one piece wrap-around grips. Two scabbard patterns are encountered with these bayonets, an all-steel stype, which is the scarcer and a leather mounted steel type. The bayonet on the right is the version with saw back blade. Although generally considered 'Pioneer' type, it was in fact issued to infantry NCOs. Blade length 20½″: overall length 25½″. *S & G Arms*

149   **150**

151

152

153

151. A Serbian Mauser bayonet, M1899. The bayonets, along with the rifles were manufactured in Germany for export to Serbia. The pommel and crossguard are made of steel, originally parkerized. The grips are twin wood slabs, secured by two countersunk nuts and bolts. The blade is single-edged, fullered on both sides and marked SIMSON, SUHL. Scabbard is steel, parkerized, with an oval frog stud situated on the face. Blade length 10″: overall length 15″. *F. J. Stephens*

152. A Mexican bayonet for the Remington Rolling Block rifle, Model 1899. These bayonets were manufactured in the United States and are marked in the blade fuller REMINGTON ARMS CO., ILION, N.Y. Twin slab wood grips are fitted to the hilt and retained in position by two bolts. The steel fittings of the hilt were originally blued, attachment to the rifle is by means of the slot and spring method and the crossguard extends into a muzzle ring (rifle cal. 7mm) and has a downswept quillon. The scabbard is made of black leather with blued steel fittings. These fittings are secured by two staples and a screw at the scabbard throat holds the scabbard retaining springs in position. A black leather frog is secured, as a permanent fixture, to the rear of the scabbard throat. Blade length 8¼″: overall length in scabbard 13½″. *Ken Holdich*

153. A Turkish Mauser knife bayonet, Model 1903. Most of the bayonets used by Turkey were manufactured in Germany, see plate 64 *Bayonets* for the model 1887: the second model adopted by Turkey was the model 1890, similar to the M1887. The illustrated example, M1903, has a steel hilt, with twin slab wood grips, secured by two countersunk bolts. A rifle slot is inset in the back of the pommel, and the bayonet attached to the rifle by means of an internal coil spring activated by a press stud set on the face

of the pommel. The steel crossguard contains a muzzle ring and has a downswept quillon. The blade is a quill-back pattern, more usually found on the M1898 German Mauser bayonets, first and second patterns. The trade mark on the ricasso of this piece is that of the firm Weyersberg, Kirschbaum & Co. of Solingen, though distinctive from its usual form in that it is written in Turkish characters. Blade length 20½″: overall length 25¾″. *S & G Arms*

154, 155. Two patterns of Model 1898/05 Mauser bayonet. These pieces have steel fittings and wood grips. The blades are short and wide, almost like a butcher's knife. The 'Pioneer' version had serrations on the blade in the centre and the regular Army issue was plain. The scabbards for these weapons are normally steel, though leather and steel versions are sometimes encountered. Blade lengths 14½″: overall lengths 19¾″. *Dr. J. Kennaugh*

154   **155**

76

156. The SMLE bayonet, Pattern 1907. Designated the Mk I bayonet, these pieces are distinctive in that they have a downswept quillon. The hilt fittings and blade are blued steel and the blade, 17″ long, has deep fullers on both sides. The grips are wood and secured by two screws. In 1913, many of these bayonets were modified by the removal of the quillon, so many were modified that the bayonet in its original state is something of a scarce collectors' item. The scabbard is leather with steel fittings. *F. J. Stephens*

157. A Ross rifle bayonet, M1910 for the Ross Rifle. The first pattern of Ross bayonet, M1905 was produced in 1907 and was distinctive in that it had a stepped crossguard, not unlike the 1888 Lee-Metford bayonet. This pattern was soon withdrawn and the Mk II (as illustrated above) was introduced. The pattern has a modified crossguard. The pommel is steel and most examples are stamped ROSS RIFLE CO. QUEBEC, PATENTED 1907. A slot, spring and press stud fixture is inset in the pommel. Twin slab wood grips are fitted, secured by two countersunk bolts and screws. The blade is straight, single-edged and unfullered. The scabbard is made of brown leather with a metal scabbard throat usually covered by a leather frog, permanently fixed by stitching. (Missing in above illustration to show the throat). The Mk II pattern of Ross bayonet was retained until 1916, when it was declared obsolete and withdrawn. *S & G Arms*

158. Ross Rifle bayonet M1910, with modified blade. The earlier examples of the Ross M1910 bayonet although having a different crossguard to the M1905 still retained the same pattern of blade, being parallel almost the whole of the length, except for the last inch where it terminated into a point. With the advent of the Great War, combat with the bayonet soon showed that this blade pattern was not of ideal design. The problem was that, on

contact in a thrust, the bayonet tended not to penetrate and was easily deflected owing to the shape of the tip. As a result, extensive modifications were carried out on all available specimens the blade being ground to a more efficient point. The example illustrated has this modification and it is unusual to find an example that has not been so treated. The scabbard shows the leather frog in the stitched position. In 1916 the Ross Rifle was withdrawn from service, as it was found unsuitable for the rough usage encountered in trench warfare. Consequently all bayonets were withdrawn and many destroyed. The United States purchased 20,000 Ross rifles and bayonets from the Canadian government, and most of these were issued to the National Guard. These bayonets were invariably overstamped with the bomb and 'US' of the American government. Blade length 10″: overall length 15″. *Ken Holdich*

156

157   158

159. A Swiss pioneer bayonet for the Schmidt-Rubin carbine of 1911. The pommel and crosspiece are of polished steel and the wooden grips secured by two rivets. The blade, which is fullered only on the right side, has a serrated back edge. The scabbard is generally of black stove-enamelled steel. Manufactured at Neuhausen, the bayonet is also found with plastic grips and a steel-mounted leather scabbard. Blade length 18¾″: overall length 24″. *F. J. Stephens*

160. The long pattern bayonet for the Danish Krag-Jørgensen rifle. The pommel, blade and crossguard are of steel, and the wooden grips are secured by two rivets. The blade, partly of T section, terminates in a double-edged tip. The scabbard is made of leather with steel mountings, a locking spring being contained in the topmount. Blade length 17¾″: overall length 22⅛″. *J. Anthony Carter*

161. An Imperial German dress bayonet, Gew. 98 pattern, with a personal emblem engraved on the pommel. The practice of marking military equipment with emblems and insignia denoting the owner was frequently done by German troops, but this practice was only permitted on 'dress' weapons—those which had been purchased at the personal expense of the owner—and not on regular service issue items. The example illustrated is a sawback pattern with a finely etched blade. The trademark clearly shown in this illustration (knight's and king's head) is that of Weyersberg, Kirchbaum & Co., arms makers of Solingen. In 1883 the companies of Weyersberg and Kirschbaum amalgamated, and for a period used both examples of their trade mark on blades as illustrated. In 1909 the mark of the knight's head came into sole use and the above 'paired' trademark was discontinued. The pommel of the illustrated bayonet is engraved with 'CS' entwined and surmounted by a crown. The grips are made of black polished and diced wood secured by three chromium-plated rivets. Although usually termed a 'dress' bayonet, the use of privately sanctioned bayonets was not favoured at official functions, and the wearing of such pieces was restricted to 'undress' or walking-out uniforms. Blade length 10″: overall length 15¼″. *Ivor F. Bush*

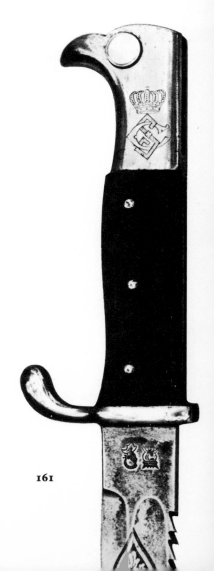

161

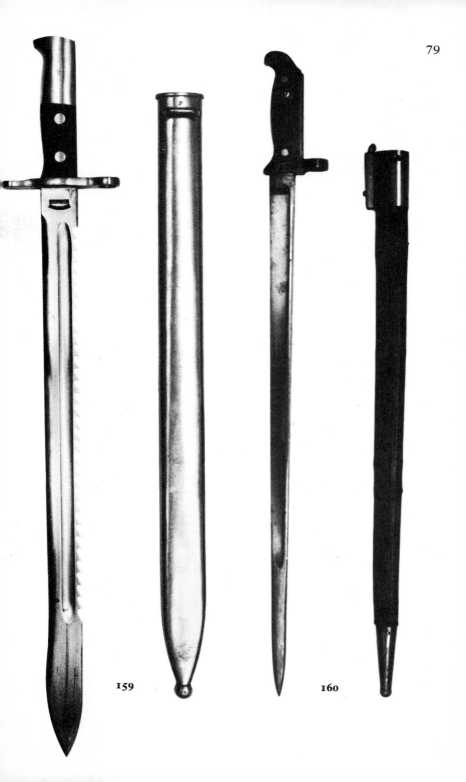

79

159   160

162

163

162. A fine presentation bayonet manufactured by Fabrique Nationale of Belgium. This bayonet was not intended to
fit any arm, but was manufactured as a
presentation piece by the FN factory. No
rifle fitment is incorporated on the piece,
and no scabbard was manufactured for it.
Complete in its presentation case, the
bayonet is finely engraved with floral
work over the pommel, crossguard and
blade. The grips are made of mother-of-
pearl, and secured by two countersunk
bolts. The floral designs of the blade
bear a panel containing the words:
FABRIQUE NATIONALE D'ARMES de
GUERRE HERSTAL BELGIQUE. Length in
case: 10″. *Tony L. Oliver*

163. A presentation bayonet manufactured by Fabrique Nationale of Belgium.
The piece illustrated is contained in its
original case, no scabbard being manufactured for it. The pommel and crossguard are nickel plated and no rifle
slotting is fitted to it: the grips are wood,
twin slab type, secured by two countersunk bolts. Inset in the right grip face is a
circular badge containing the letters FN.
The blade is straight, with a simulated
edge and false-edge. The flat of the blade
is engraved: FABRIQUE NATIONALE D'
ARMES DE GUERRE HERSTAL BELGIQUE.
Overall length in case: 10″. *Tony L. Oliver*

164. A Greek knife bayonet for the
Mannlicher-Schönauer rifle, Model
1903.
The hilt and crossguard are made of
steel, with press stud and spring inset in
the pommel, and a rifle slot. The grips are
wood, twin slab type, and secured by
means of two countersunk bolts. The
blade is straight and single-edged with a
double-edged tip, and 'T' shape in
cross-section.
The scabbard (not illustrated) is steel,
and has a blued finish. Blade length $15\frac{1}{2}$″:
overall length 20″. *Herman A. Maeurer*

165. A Greek knife bayonet for the
Mannlicher-Schönauer rifle, Model
1903. The hilt is identical in size and
style to the previously illustrated piece,
having twin slab wood grips secured by
two countersunk bolts. The blade is
straight and double-edged, without fullering but has the suggestion of a broad
high ridge running along the centre. The
scabbard is steel, with a frog stud brazed
to the body below the throat. The
scabbard finish can be either blued steel
or stove-enamelled black. Both of the
previously illustrated patterns were in
service throughout both World Wars.
Blade length $9\frac{1}{2}$″: overall length 14″.
Herman A. Maeurer

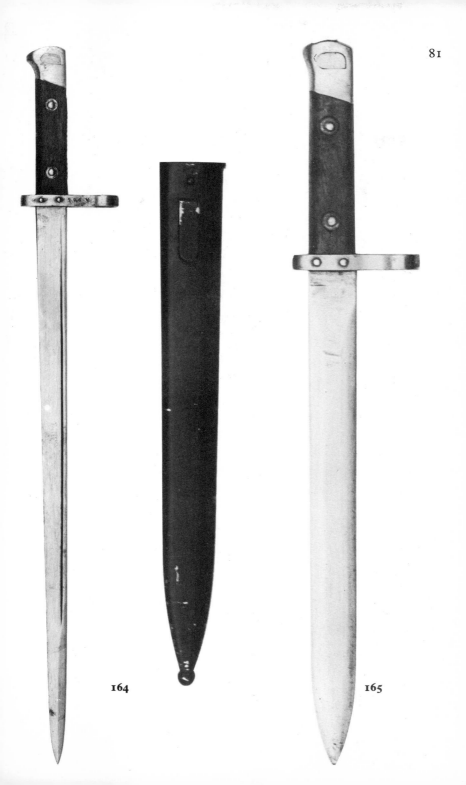

164

165

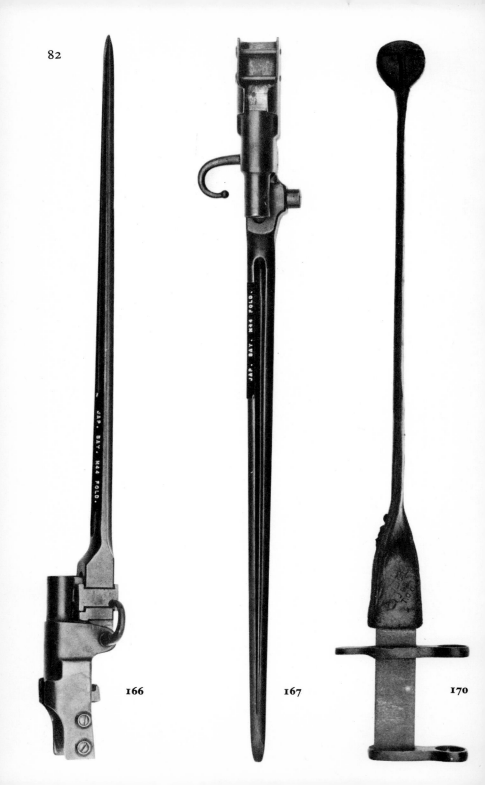

82

166

167

170

166, 167. The Japanese Type 44 (1911) folding bayonet, for the Arisaka carbine Type 44 and also used during World War II. Officially the bayonet was issued for use with the 6.5mm Cavalry Carbine of 1911. No scabbard was issued with the bayonet, as it was intended to be a permanent feature of the arm to which it was attached, and was secured to the weapon by means of two bolts which passed through the wood stock. Muzzle fixture was by means of a tube. It is interesting to observe that a hooked quillon was incorporated in the design. The blade has a screwdriver tip and is fullered on both sides. Blade length 14″: overall length 19″. *Herman A. Maeurer*

168. An imperial German Trench dagger/bayonet. Probably dating from the First World War, this piece is perfectly standard in style, except for the modification of the grip and the grip emblem. This could have been a lapel badge, but its position may be contemporary with the manufacture of the piece. The emblem, it has been suggested, is probably Hungarian, though its identification and reference have not as yet been located. *Photograph by John Burden*

169. A combination trench knife/bayonet, German, dating from World War I. Small and compact, this bayonet is made of steel; the short blade is straight and double-edged and the recurving hilt has steel grips secured to the tang by four rivets. Blade length 6″: overall length 10¼″. *Ivor F. Bush*

170. The American training bayonet, used on the Fencing Musket model 1915 by military cadets of the West Point Academy. Attachment to the fencing musket is simply by means of twin muzzle rings fitted to the hilt. The blade is a flat spring-steel unit, covered with leather and terminating in a loop. It is, of course, a safety feature intended to

prevent accidental penetration during practice. It was manufactured by the Rock Island Arsenal. Blade length 16″: overall length 19″. *Herman A. Maeurer*

168   169

84

171

172

173

174

175

176

177

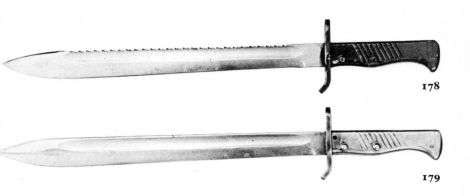

178

179

171. A World War I Austrian *ersatz* bayonet. Made for the M1888 Mannlicher rifle, these crudely constructed bayonets were produced during periods of shortage in 1917–8. Distinctive with their absence of grips, these ingeniously designed pieces were so constructed as to fit on the standard bayonet bar on the Mannlicher rifles. Blade length 10¼″: overall length 14¼″. *R. D. C. Evans*

172. A variation of the *ersatz* bayonet issued by the Austrians to fit the M1888 Mannlicher rifle, this example has, however, a heavy 12¾″ blade. The scabbard is made of sheet zinc. Overall length 17¾″. *R. D. C. Evans*

173, 174. Two variations of the *ersatz* all-steel German bayonet of World War I. The item on the left (173) has a flat steel hilt and an extended barrel ring with single edged blade which is fullered on both sides. The scabbard in the centre is a typical pattern that was issued with many variations of the *ersatz* weapons.

The bayonet on the right (174) is another variation having a grooved steel hilt and no barrel ring. The blade is straight and unfullered. All blades of these types of bayonet average 12″ in length and overall length average 17″. *Ken Holdich*

175, 176, 177. Three imperial German *ersatz* bayonets of all metal construction. The model on the left has a brass hilt and the examples on the right are steel hilted. The bayonets were designed to fit the Gew. 88 Commission rifle and the Gew. 98. Blade lengths approximately 12″: overall lengths 17″. *R. D. C. Evans*

178, 179. Two imperial German *ersatz* M1898/05 bayonets. Of all-metal construction, the left version—with sawback—blade is the more common pattern. The standard blade on the right was very rarely attached to this type of hilt. The scabbards for these pieces are also of steel construction. Blade length 14″: overall length 19″. *R. D. C. Evans*

181

182

183

180. A German *ersatz* bayonet, produced during World War I. The hilt is brass, grooved at an angle of approximately 40° in the portion normally containing the grips. A spring release press stud and rifle slot is incorporated in the pommel and three steel rivets secure the solid brass hilt to the tang. Towards the crossguard an oiling hole is drilled, the purpose of this being to prevent corrosion attacking the tang of the blade and the securing rivets. The blade is cruciform in cross-section. The scabbard is steel, tubular and tapered. Blade length $17\frac{1}{2}''$: overall length $22\frac{1}{4}''$. *R. D. C. Evans*

181, 182, 183. Three German World War I *ersatz* bayonets of all-steel construction. That on the left is the most common example, those in the centre and on the right are almost identical except that the centre piece has a $\frac{3}{4}''$

barrel ring, enabling the bayonet to be fitted to captured Lebel or Mosin-Nagant rifles by means of an adaptor. All blade lengths $12''$. *R. D. C. Evans*

184. A German manufactured knife bayonet, originally made as an export item for South America. During World War I the urgent need for bayonets necessitated the issuing of this pattern to German forces and it appears to have been notably used by machine-gunners with the Kar. 98. The hilt is steel, with twin slab wood grips ribbed on the face edge and secured by two countersunk bolts. No muzzle ring is incorporated in the design, but the quillon is of up-swept type. The blade is straight, single-edged and fullered on both sides. It is known that a variation pattern with saw-back blade was issued to pioneer troops. Blade length $14\frac{1}{2}''$: overall length $19\frac{3}{4}''$. *Ken Holdich*

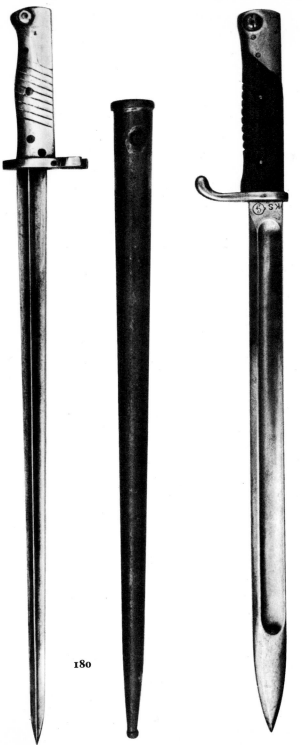

180

184

185   186   188

185. The American-manufactured bayonet for the Pattern 1914 Enfield rifle. This bayonet was also used on the Winchester and Remington riot shotguns, as well as the M1917 Enfield rifle which was used by American troops during World War I. It was manufactured for the rifle in the British .303″ calibre and US .30–06″ calibre, and also the .276″ calibre Pederson rifle. The blade is single-edged and fullered on both sides. The ricasso is stamped with the manufacturer and date—REMINGTON 1917. The whole of the blade and the hilt fittings were originally blued, and the grips are two wooden slabs with two grooves across the width. They are retained in position by two countersunk bolts. An oiling hole is drilled in the face of the pommel, and fixture to the rifle is by means of the slot and spring method. The scabbard is made of black leather and has blued steel fittings stapled to the body. Blade length 17″: overall length 22″. *Ken Holdich*

186. The Belgian Mauser bayonet, M1916. This bayonet was adopted for use by the Belgian Infantry in 1916, and was designed to fit the Mauser rifle, Model 1889. The bayonet has an overall length of 22⅜″, with a blade length of 17⅝″. The pommel is fitted with a rifle slot and contains a locking spring, operated by a press stud situated on the left face of the pommel. The grips are made of wood and secured to the hilt by means of two countersunk bolts, which pass through the tang of the blade, and are secured by means of two nuts which fit flush with the surface of the rear grip. The crossguard extends to a barrel ring (17.5mm diameter), no quillon being incorporated in the design of this crossguard. The blade of the bayonet is double-edged and is roughly finished, the coarse surface finish being original to the manufacture of the bayonet. The whole of the metal work of this piece is heavily blued. The scabbard (not illustrated) is made of blued steel, and tapers to a small boss at the tip. Two screws situated on the front and rear of the scabbard secure the blade retaining springs. Suspension of the scabbard in the frog is by means of an elongated frog stud placed just below the throat.

In 1924 Belgium adopted the new Mauser M1924, which was manufactured by Fabrique Nationale. The bayonet designed to fit this rifle was almost identical to the M1916, but can be identified by the smaller diameter of the barrel ring (15mm). The scabbard of this later bayonet also differs, having two rivets placed in place of the spring screws at the scabbard throat. Like the M1916, the bayonet M1924 is heavily blued. *F. J. Stephens*

187. An Imperial German Trench dagger/bayonet, c. 1916. This weapon was manufactured by Deutsche Maschinenfabrik A-G, of Duisburg, and was the subject of a patent applied for by the makers. Intended to serve both as a bayonet and a trench dagger as need be, it has steel pommel with twin slab wood grips. The blade is single-edged with a short false edge at the tip. A steel scabbard with riveted leather frog was attached to the back of the throat. Blade length 6⅛″: overall length 10¾″. *R. D. C. Evans*

188. A Swedish bayonet, c. 1917 for the modification of the M1894 Swedish Mauser Carbine. The original 1894 rifle had no provision for a bayonet, but in 1917 existing supplies of the carbine were modified to permit use of a bayonet and the type shown above was designed to fit it. Blade length 13″: overall length 18″. *R. D. C. Evans*

187

189. A German trench knife/bayonet. This small piece, which has the blade etched with SOUVENIR OF SOLINGEN, was probably manufactured after World War I, and sold as a tourist item. The practice of modifying unissued stocks of bayonets and making new fancy patterns was quite widespread after the first war, and served both as a method of disposing of the stocks of such weapons of war and as a revenue source. Blade length $5\frac{1}{2}''$: overall length $10\frac{3}{8}''$. *R. D. C. Evans*

190. A German bayonet-type trench dagger, produced after World War I. Many variations are encountered in this type of weapon, some of which are made exactly like bayonets complete with locking slots, others with an immovable press stud but no slot (as illustrated above), and others without any bayonet characteristics. The collector encountering these may be bewildered why a bayonet should be made that is unsuitable for use on any rifle. The reason is that after World War I German arms makers were severely restricted in the manufacture of weapons for military use. Consequently many unusual bayonet-type knives were produced, which were sold as export items or as tourist souvenirs. The hilt of the illustrated example was originally chrome plated and the grips are black chequered plastic secured by two rivets. The blade is straight, double-edged and unfullered, while the scabbard is of pressed steel, stove enamelled black. Blade length $6''$: overall length $10\frac{1}{2}''$. *Ken Holdich*

191. A Weimarian Service bayonet Seitengewehr M1884/98. This example is quite similar to the standard service issue used during the Second World War, but differs in that it has black chequered grips, which are manufactured from a hard rubber compound. The grips are secured to the hilt by two smooth bolts, which pass through the grips and tang, and are held secure by two circular nuts (slotted for machine tightening) on the reverse side. On both grips the bolts and nuts are countersunk flush with the grip surface. The hilt is steel, and finished with a matt blue surface. Attachment to the rifle is by means of a spring securing device set in the rifle slot in the back-edge of the pommel. Release is by means of a spring loaded press stud. The blade of the bayonet is single-edged, and fullered on both sides. The scabbard (not illustrated) is steel. Blade length $10''$: overall length $15\frac{1}{4}''$. *R. D. C. Evans*

192. A Belgian made knife bayonet for the F.N. export Mauser rifle, Models 1924, 24–30 and 1934. Among the countries which used this pattern were Persia, Ethiopia, Paraguay and Uruguay. The pommel and crossguard are polished steel and twin wood slab grips are fitted: the polished steel blade is single-edged, with fullers on both sides. The scabbard is made of steel, stove-enamelled black and with an elongated frog stud brazed to the face. Blade length $11\frac{5}{8}''$: overall length $16\frac{7}{8}''$. *Ken Holdich*

189

190   191   192

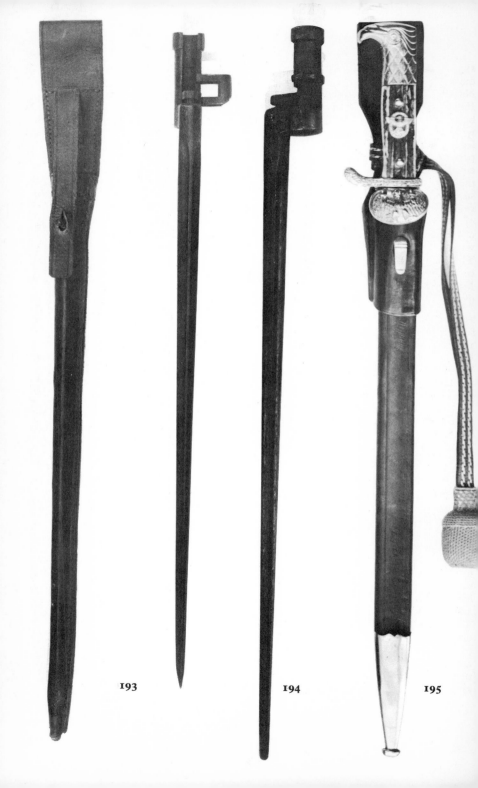

193 194 195

193. Finnish Mosin-Nagant socket bayonet, Model 1891/30. The Mosin-Nagant rifle was the standard arm of the Finnish soldier until about 1960. The bayonet illustrated has a cruciform blade, with elbowed open-side socket. The foresight guard is intended as an integral part of the weapon, though it is in fact constructed separately and attached to the socket by means of a screw. The scabbard is black leather, stitched on the reverse side. Suspension and securing of the bayonet when carried was by means of a leather frog, which carried a thong wrapped over the socket of the bayonet. The bayonet, heavily blued, was intended for use on the 7.62mm Mosin-Nagant Model 1891/30 rifle. Blade length 17": overall length 19". *Herman A. Maeurer*

194. A Soviet Russian socket bayonet for the Mosin-Nagant rifle, model 1891/30. Although considered as just the M91/30, it was used throughout World War II and remained in general service until about 1947.

The whole of the bayonet is steel and heavily blued. The blade is cruciform in cross-section, terminating in a screw-driver tip; this enabled the bayonet to be used as a stripping tool for the rifle. Blade length 17": overall length 20". *S & G Arms*

195. A Nazi Police bayonet, the first pattern, of 1933. This bayonet is in fact a Weimarian piece, but upon the formation of the Nazi Government in 1933, the Weimarian eagle emblem which previously was set in the grip, was replaced by the new Nazi Police emblem—an eagle and swastika set over an oval of oak leaves. The pommel is nickel-plated, and cut in the form of an eagle's head. The single upswept quillon also bears an oak leaf design, and the Eagle of Weimar ornates the shell guard. The grips are made of stag horn, secured by two nickel-plated rivets which pass through the grips and the tang of the blade. The

scabbard of this example is brown leather, with nickel-plated steel fittings. Attachment to the belt of the wearer is by means of the brown leather frog (the *Portepee* knot shown in the illustration is not original). This bayonet has a 17" blade, but this was made obsolete by preference to the shorter 9⅞" blade shortly after adoption in 1933. Further modifications were made to the Police bayonet by removing the shell guard on the later patterns. To comply with this new modification some examples of the bayonet simply had the shell guard cut away, whereas the later patterns were manufactured without it. *Wallis & Wallis*

196

197

196, 197. A close-up view of the grip emblems of the Weimarian Republic Police bayonet. On the left is the standard Weimarian pattern, a six-sided sunburst with the Eagle of Weimar. Right: a modification introduced after the Nazis came to power, carried only by members of the Feldjäger Police, the Prussian Police and the Hermann Göring special police units from the Lichterfelde cadet school. The emblem is again a six-sided sunburst, with a flighted eagle, swastika on breast, carrying a sword and lightning flashes. This latter pattern was retained in service until c. 1935 when it was made obsolescent and a new pattern of bayonet authorised for wear. The new pattern had been standard issue for all other police units since 1934. *F. J. Stephens & B. Smith*

198. A German Land Customs bayonet, c. 1934. This example has a standard pattern 'dress' bayonet blade, $9\frac{7}{8}''$ in length: the hilt is nickel-plated, and has the pommel decorated in relief in the form of an eagle's head. The single upswept quillon is ornated with oak leaves, and surmounts a shell guard which bears a German eagle of Wei-

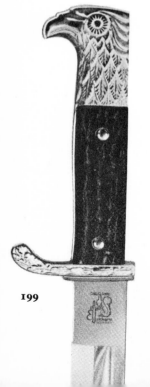

199

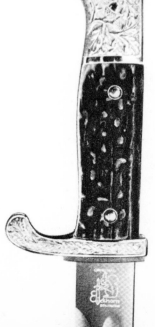

200

marian style, no swastika being incorporated in the design. The grips are made of staghorn and secured to the hilt by means of two nickel-plated rivets which pass through the tang of the blade. The scabbard is steel and stove-enamelled black. *Wallis & Wallis*

199. A Nazi German Land Customs Officials' dress bayonet. This pattern is of the same dimensions as the standard Wehrmacht dress bayonet (9⅞" blade), but differs in having a decorated pommel and quillon rather like that found on the police bayonets. The grip is made of staghorn and the scabbard is metal with black leather body. All metal portions are nickel-plated. Officials of the Water Customs were permitted to wear a variation 'dress' bayonet which had a shell guard somewhat similar to that of the Weimarian Police bayonets, but without the grip emblem. The metal portions of the Water Customs bayonet were gilded and the scabbard body was made of black leather. *Eikhorn Kundendienst*

200. A de-luxe pattern dress bayonet for 'dress' wear by all personnel—if desired—of the Army, Navy and Luftwaffe. Like all dress bayonets the wear of this pattern was optional, and it was slightly more expensive to buy than the standard patterns of dress bayonet. The whole of the metal work is nickel-plated, and ornated in relief with acorns and oak leaves. Sometimes this bayonet is mistakenly classified as an 'Honour' bayonet, which is only partly true. Examples of this nature were sometimes given as prizes or honorary awards for proficiency in some aspect concerned with extra-curricula activities, but it was also quite permissible to purchase the bayonet privately. As with the standard patterns of dress bayonet the scabbard was black stove-enamelled steel. Blade length 9⅞".
Eickhorn Kundendienst

198

201

3219

3220

3221

3222

3223/3220

3227/3220

3228/3221

3229/3219

202 –10

201. A manufacturer's illustration of the blade etching which might accompany a deluxe version 'dress' bayonet when presented as a 'honorary' award or prize. In the illustrated case it applies to marksmanship, the blade bearing an etched panel with blued background, accompanied by the dedication DEM BESTEN SCHUTZEN. 13/INF. REGT. 61. *Eickhorn Kundendienst*

202–210. A selection of etched bayonet blades which could be purchased privately for wear on 'dress' bayonets. Many bore the dedication ZUR ERINNERUNG AN MEINE DIENSTZEIT (In memory of my military service) and it was often the practice of personnel to buy,

or to be presented with, such dedicated pieces on retirement from active service, and to wear them thereafter at Old Comrades' reunions. Also available were emblems denoting the branch of service in which they served, such as Infantry, Tank Corps or Flak Units. Other variations in blade etchings show scenes of Cavalry charges, Regimental Titles and, occasionally, the personal name of the owner. *Eickhorn Kundendienst*

211–215. A further selection of etching patterns for dress bayonets, included in the designs illustrated above are some that would be chosen by Luftwaffe personnel. *Eickhorn Kundendienst*

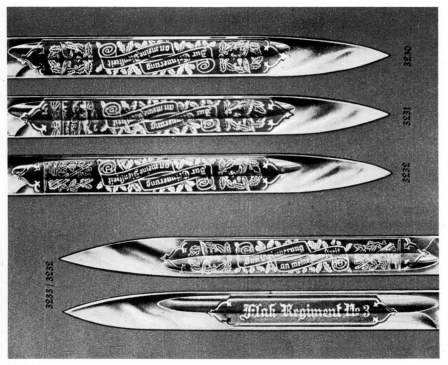

211–15

98

216   217   219   218

216. A French spike bayonet for the MAS rifle, M1936. Manufactured by *Manufacture d'Armes de St. Etienne* (MAS), this bayonet was designed to be carried at all times on the rifle, as no scabbards were ever produced. The blade is cruciform in cross section while the hilt is tubular with a knurled centre band and bears two locking clips, which operate by means of a spring. When not intended for use the bayonet was retained on the rifle in the reverse position with the blade facing towards the breech. The bayonet was used on the 7.5mm MAS rifle M1936, and the M36 CR39 rifle which had a folding aluminium stock. Blade length 13½″: overall length 17″. *Herman A. Maeurer*

217. The bayonet for the Swiss Favor sub-machine-gun. Similar to the French MAS 1936 bayonet, the Favor is shorter and the section blade is circular rather than cruciform. The method of attachment is identical, using two spring catches and when the bayonet is not in use it is carried in the reversed position. The bayonet is fitted to the compensator attached to the muzzle. The whole of the bayonet and compensator are parkerized a deep blue-grey. As a bayonet the Favor, like the MAS, is suitable only as a thrusting weapon. For bayonet service this is ideal, though in terms of the more traditional weapon of the knife or sword bayonet it has no value. Blade length 9⅛″: overall length 11⅜″. *S & G Arms*

218. The Favor bayonet shown attached to the compensator. *R. D. C. Evans*

219. A Swiss 9mm parabellum experimental Favor sub-machine-gun with the compensator device manufactured as an integral part of the barrel. The Favor spike bayonet is shown fixed to the arm. *Weller & Dufty*

220. A variant of the Nazi dress bayonet. Of the three basic patterns manufactured, this is the rarest: compared to the more common varieties the piece differs only in the absence of the upswept quillon and 'eagle's beak' pommel. At the time of manufacture, the prices of the three basic patterns of dress bayonet were the same and it appears that, because this style did not conform with the general trend towards 'eagle's head' patterns, it never became popular, being today a rare pattern. The hilt is chromed and there are chequered plastic grips, it is of the same dimensions as the usual variations. *F. J. Stephens*

220

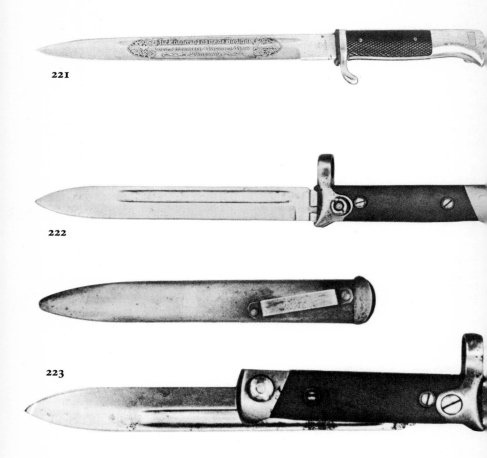

221

222

223

221. A Nazi 'dress' bayonet with a dedicated blade. The 'dress' bayonet was not standard service issue, but had to be purchased privately by the wearer. For extra payment it was possible to have the blade etched with any form of decoration, wording or dedication. The illustrated example, which bears the trade mark of Puma-Werke of Solingen, is etched with a panel containing an eagle and swastika (at the tip end of the etching) and a Wehrmacht steel helmet (Ricasso end of the panel) with the dedication

Zur Errinerrung an meine Dienstzeit beim Infantrie Regiment No. 47 Lüneburg—In memory of my Military Service, in Infantry Regiment No. 47, Lüneburg. The hilt of the bayonet is nickel-plated and has black plastic grips, with a chequered surface. The grips are secured to the hilt by means of two nickel-plated rivets passing through the tang of the blade. A rifle locking slot, with spring release press stud is incorporated in the pommel. The overall length of the bayonet is the same as the standard pattern long dress bayonet. Scabbard (not illustrated) is steel, stove-enamelled black. Blade length $9\frac{7}{8}"$: overall length $14\frac{3}{4}"$ *R. D. C. Evans*

222. An Italian bayonet for the Model 1938 Mannlicher-Carcano rifle. This bayonet has a folding blade and, although issued with a scabbard for wear, the original intention was for the bayonet to be carried at all times on the rifle with the blade folded when not required. Blade length $6\frac{3}{4}"$: overall length $11\frac{1}{4}"$. *R. D. C. Evans*

223. The M1938 Mannlicher-Carcano bayonet shown in the folded position. *R. D. C. Evans*

224. A German M84/98 of Nazi manufacture. This pattern of bayonet had been in regular use since World War I and, with minor modifications, continued in service until the end of World War II. Up to 1937 wood grips were fitted to this pattern, and thereafter bakelite grips became the standard feature. The pommel and blade are blued, and the bakelite grips are secured by two countersunk bolts. The pressed steel scabbard was originally blued and has an elongated frog stud brazed to the front of the scabbard. Suspension is by means of a black leather frog. Generally speaking the bayonet is considered strictly a military item used by all branches of the Wehrmacht—it was, however, also issued in certain cases to Allegemeine SS (Political para-military organisation), Waffen-SS (Military Arm of the SS), SA Wehrmann (Political SA personnel who assisted with the war effort by guarding factories, prisoners and general assistance for which able-bodied males males were not available due to war service). This latter groups' activities were soon replaced by the Hitler Youth units (from *c.* 1942). Blade length $10"$: overall length $15\frac{1}{4}"$. *Ken Holdich*

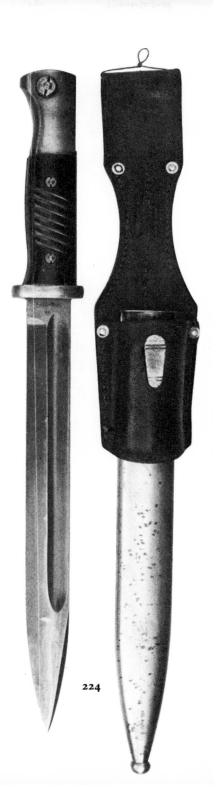

224

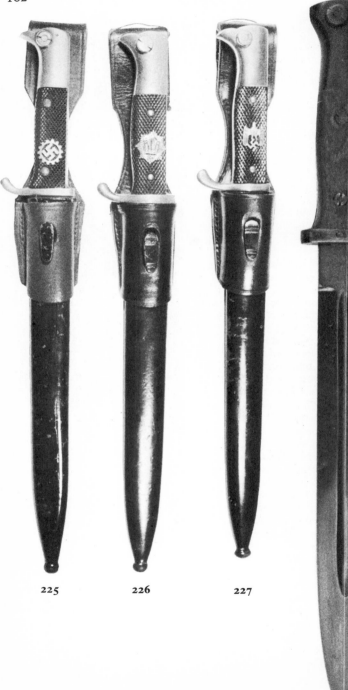

225 226 227 230

Three German dress bayonets bearing emblems of the services in which they were carried. Such pieces were manufactured only for a short period during the early years of the Third Reich. (See *The Daggers and Edged Weapons of Hitler's Germany*, by Major James P. Atwood.)

225. Dress bayonet bearing the cogwheel and swastika of DAF (Deutsche Arbeit Fronte), the German Workers' Front, an organisation which concerned itself with the manufacture of munitions.

226. Reichsluftschutz Bund dress bayonet, the Reich Air Defence organisation.

227. A standard Wehrmacht dress bayonet with inset emblem. *F. J. Stephens— B. Smith*

228. An American bayonet for the M1 Garand automatic rifle. This particular specimen has been shortened from the M1942 knife bayonet, although newly manufactured blades were used from 1943. The new blades can be recognised by the shorter fullers rather than the full-length grooving. The Plastic grips are secured with a single screwbolt. The scabbard has a metal top mount and an olive green plastic body. *Ken Holdich*

229. An Australian prototype machete bayonet, Model 1943: approximately 600 of which were manufactured. The pommel and crosspiece are blued steel and the bolo-type blade, which is double-edged at the tip, is also blued. The grips are wood secured by two screws. The scabbard for this bayonet is made of canvas webbing. Blade length $11\frac{1}{4}$": overall length $16\frac{1}{8}$". *J. Anthony Carter*

230. A Spanish-manufactured Mauser bayonet, M1943. These bayonets were manufactured in Spain for use with the Spanish Mauser rifle. They are almost identical to their German-made counterparts except that they are made with wood grips and the overall construction of the bayonet is inferior to that of the German-made versions. This can be easily detected by the collector who will, on examination, note that the blades of such examples are usually slimmer (0.9") and only 9" long. German patterns tended to be slightly longer. Owing to the poor workmanship the blades of these Spanish pieces are frequently seen to be bent. The scabbard is made of pressed steel and the throat is manufactured without a lip, a feature always found on the German specimens. All the metal portions of the bayonets are blued. Blade length 9": overall length $14\frac{3}{4}$". *Ken Holdich*

231. The Spanish Mauser bayonet shown attached to the German Kar 98 rifle. The bayonet is almost identical to the German made versions, but can be identified from the German made patterns by quality of manufacture. *S & G Arms*

228

229

231

232

232. An unusual device for repelling an adversary—en entrenching tool with a bayonet attachment. The illustration shows a feature almost unique in the service of the bayonet, fixture to a device other than a firearm. As seen above, a British Army entrenching tool with removable spade/pick head, can be fitted with a bayonet (on the example shown a No. 4 Mk. I). This fitting will also accommodate a No. 9 (bowie blade) socket bayonet. *R. D. C. Evans*

233. The entrenching tool shown with the bayonet fixed. *R. D. C. Evans*

234. An unidentified Swedish knife bayonet. This has a steel hilt with wooden

grips, and a steel scabbard. It is believed that this is the bayonet for the AG42 (Ljungmann) semi-automatic rifle of 1942. Blade length $8\frac{1}{4}''$: overall length $12\frac{1}{2}''$. *R. D. C. Evans*

235, 236, 237, 238. Four variations of the United States M8 and M8A1 scabbard, as issued with such bayonets as the M4, M5 and M7. All the scabbards are made of green coloured plastic-like material with a webbing frog. All have an eyelet at the tip, the original purpose of which was to thread with a length of leather thong for tying the scabbard tip to the leg of the wearer. *Drawings by M. H. Cole*

233

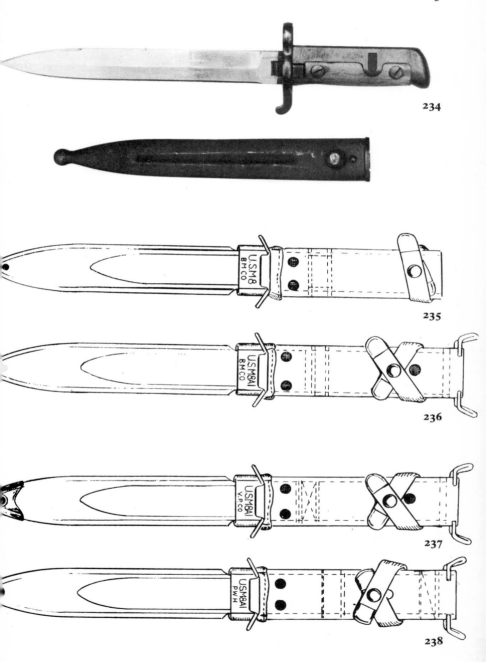

234

235

236

237

238

239   241

239, 240. An American bayonet for the Johnson semi-automatic rifle of 1943. The bayonet is of all steel construction, parkerized overall and the blade is triangular in cross-section without cutting edges. The hilt is most distinctive being constructed solely as a locking device for the rifle. The scabbard is brown leather with a leather frog stitched to the body. Two patterns of the bayonet are said to exist, one with a 16″ sword blade, and short pattern as above. Blade length 8″: overall length 12″. *F. J. Stephens*

241. An American training bayonet, used by the United States Navy. Designated Mk. I, pattern 1943, for use on the 1903 dummy training rifle. About 300,000 of these training bayonets were manufactured and then declared obsolete because they were considered too dangerous. The blade is laminated steel covered with black plastic. Blade length 15⅞″: overall length 20½″. *R. D. C. Evans*

242. An Australian bayonet, for the Owen sub-machine gun Model 1944. There is a blued steel pommel and crosspiece, and the blade, which is straight is single-edged and fullered. The grips are wood with two securing screws and the scabbard is blued metal. Blade length 10″: overall length 14¾″. *J. Anthony Carter*

243. British Bayonet No. 5 Mk. II for the Jungle carbine. Two variations of this bayonet exist, the No. 5 Mk. I (introduced 12th September, 1944) was distinctive in that it had the grips secured with one nut and bolt; the No. 5 Mk. II —as illustrated has the grips secured by two bolts (introduced early in 1945). The hilt is steel, heavily parkerized, with twin slab wood grips. The blade is straight, single-edged (double-edged at tip) and bowie shaped. The scabbard is steel, parkerized, and suspension by means of a webbing frog attached to a circular frog stud situated on the scabbard face. Blade length 7¾″: overall length 10¼″. *Ken Holdich*

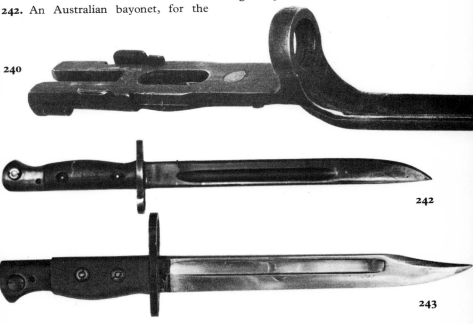

240

242

243

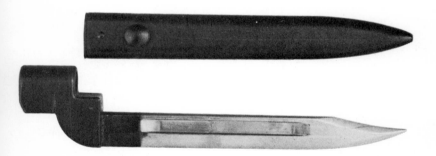

244

245

246

249

248

247

244. The No. 7 bayonet. This has a socket fixture with plastic grips secured by two countersunk bolts. The blade is the same as the No. 5 pattern, as is the scabbard. An interesting feature of this bayonet is that the pommel has to be swivelled to accommodate the rifle. *Ken Holdich*

245. The No. 7 bowie blade bayonet, showing the pommel in the swivelled position ready for fixture to the rifle. Blade length 7¾″: overall length 12¼″. *Ken Holdich*

246. A No. 9 bowie blade socket bayonet. This bayonet has a socket fitting similar to the No. 4 spike bayonet, but the blade is a bowie pattern, identical in length to the No. 5 bayonet. The No. 9 was mainly issued to the Royal Navy with the No. 4 rifle. The scabbard is the same as that of the No. No. 5. Blade length 8″: overall length 10¼″. *Ken Holdich*

247, 248, 249. To supplement the sup-ply of bayonets to Indian troops during World War II the manufacturing of bayonets commenced at the arsenals of Ishapore and Ferozepore in 1942. The rigours of economy production and the demands of wartime governments inevitably result in the production of items that are identical only in principle, and varied because of the restrictions of the day. As a result of the demands of war time production, the India pattern Lee-Enfield bayonet exists in a number of distinct variations: No. 1 Mk. I, identical to the Pattern 1907 bayonet without quillon. No. 1 Mk. I★, as the above item, but with the blade shortened from 17″ to 12″. No. 1 Mk. II, the same hilt type as above, but manufactured with 12″ blade with no fullers (247); No. 1 Mk. II★, identical to Mk. II but having false edge on blade tip (248); No. 1 Mk. III, 12″ unfullered blade, no false edge, square hilt. No. 1 Mk. III, 12″ unfullered blade, with false edge and a square hilt (249). Introduced in 1945. Blade length 12″: overall length 16¾″. *Ken Holdich*

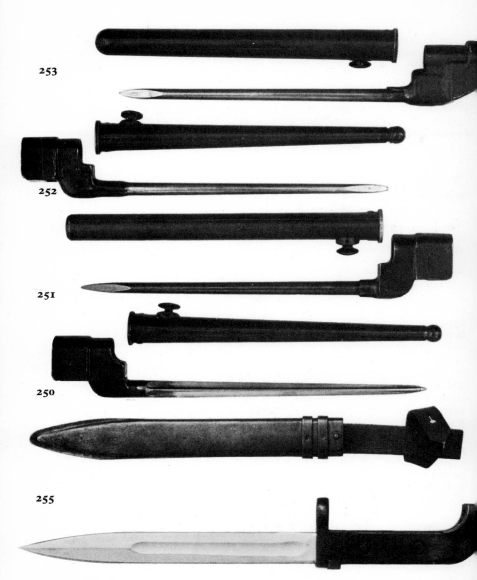

250, 251, 252, 253. Assorted spike bayonets for the No. 4 rifle. These bayonets are socket bayonets with a locking spring and catch contained within the socket. Experiments with spike bayonets for British troops were being tried in 1925, but it was not until 15th November 1939 that the first pattern was offiically approved. The first accepted pattern was designated the No. 4 bayonet Mk. I (250). This bayonet had a cruciform blade and the scabbard manufactured for the bayo-

net was tapered. In 1940 a modified version of the bayonet was produced and designated the No. 4 Mk. II: this bayonet (251) mainly differed in having a blade that was circular in cross-section and the tip was of screwdriver pattern. The whole of the socket, shoulder and bayonet were cast in a single piece. Originally the bayonet was issued with a tapered scabbard, but these were withdrawn in 1943 when a straight design of scabbard was issued. The No. 4 Mk. II* spike bayonet was introduced in 1941. The bayonet (252) was similar to the Mk. II, except that the blade was manufactured separately to the socket and shoulder and then brazed on to it. This bayonet was also originally issued with the tapered scabbard, but then replaced with a straight scabbard. The last spike bayonet was the crudely made Mk. III (253).
Ken Holdich

254. The Soviet Russian Mosin Nagant folding bayonet, Model 1944. This bayonet is intended to be an integral part of the Mosin-Nagant carbine, and is normally a permanent feature of the weapon. When not in use it is folded back along the stock of the arm and, when fixed, folded forward. Locking was by means of a barrel ring fitted to a spring loaded collar, normally fixed to the tang of the blade. The bayonet pivots on a stud projection by means of the hole in the tang and, when required for service, the collar and barrel ring attach to the barrel and retain the bayonet securely.

The blade is cruciform in cross-section, and has a screwdriver tip. The whole of the bayonet is blued and, as it was intended to be retained on the arm at all times, no scabbard was ever made. Blade length 12½": overall length 15".
Herman A. Maeurer

255. The Soviet Russian bayonet for the 7.62mm calibre Russian Assault Rifle AK 47. (Avtomat Kalashnikov '47). This bayonet is current Soviet issue and

exists in two versions—one with a folding metal stock, the other with a fixed stock as illustrated. The grips are of a mauve coloured plastic substance, and the blade finish is rather like that of satin-chrome. The scabbard is pressed steel and suspension is by means of a webbing frog riveted through the twin bands at the throat. *S & G Arms*

254

256

257

258

256. A bayonet for the Belgian FN Model ABL semi-automatic rifle, 1949. The hilt metal portions are polished steel, with twin slab wood grips secured by means of two countersunk nuts and bolts. The blade is double-edged and not unlike the British 1888 Lee-Metford blades. The scabbard is steel and parkerized. The rifles and bayonets were manufactured as export items and were sold mainly to the governments of Egypt and Venezuela. Blade length $9\frac{1}{16}''$: overall length $14\frac{1}{4}''$. *R. D. C. Evans*

257. The American M4 bayonet/knife of 1944. It was designed to fit the Carbine M1, 1941. The grip of this particular pattern of bayonet is built up of brown leather washers and the scabbard designated M8AI, (as is the M7 bayonet scabbard). Blade length $6\frac{3}{4}''$: overall length $11\frac{5}{8}''$. *R. D. C. Evans*

258. A Venezuelan Mauser bayonet, Model 1949. The pommel and crosspiece are polished steel and there is a straight single-edged fullered blade. The grips are wood, secured by two screws. Manufactured in Belgium. Blade length $15\frac{1}{4}''$: overall length $20\frac{3}{8}''$. *J. Anthony Carter*

259. A Danish knife bayonet, M1947 for the Madsen rifles, M1947 and M1947/53. The bayonets were also used by Brazil, Thailand, Indonesia, Chile and Guatemala. The hilt is parkerized steel, and twin slab wood grips are fitted: the blade is straight, double-edged and unfullered. The scabbard is especially interesting in manufacture, being constructed from a tube, pressed flat in a die and brazed at the seams. The throat is banded and a circular frog stud is fixed to the face of the scabbard. The whole of the scabbard is parkerized black. Blade length $8\frac{1}{4}''$: overall length $12\frac{3}{4}''$. *F. J. Stephens*

260. A folding bayonet for the Patchett Sub-machine gun, c. 1952. The Patchett was the forerunner to the Sterling and, during the test period of the gun, this design of bayonet was experimentally used with it. The bayonet was modified from the blade of a No. 5 Mk. II bayonet, the hilt having been removed and a swivel fitted to the tang—which has been shortened. Brazed to the back edge of the blade is a spring-contained locking device, which mated with a corresponding portion on the underside of the barrel. When not in use the bayonet folded to a position with the tip to the rear. As far as is known the bayonet in this form was never adopted, the final version of the gun, the Sterling, being fitted with a modified version of the No. 5 Mk. II bayonet, the same blade as this illustrated, but different method of attachment. Overall length $8\frac{1}{4}''$. *S & G Arms*

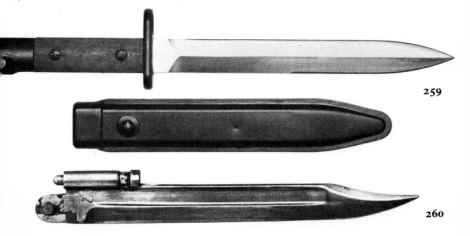

259

260

261. A Belgian knife bayonet *c.* 1954, for the 7.62mm NATO FN FAL Assault rifle. The bayonet exists in several patterns which have been exported to various countries, and grips are to be found of sheet metal as well as wood. The example illustrated has sheet metal grips, secured by two countersunk bolts. A rifle slot and spring is set in the pommel, being released by a retractable loop attached to the spring mechanism shown projecting from the pommel. The whole of the bayonet is parkerized and no flash eliminator is incorporated in the muzzle ring. The blade is straight, and double-edged at the tip, with no fullering. *S & G Arms*

262. A Belgian-manufactured FN bayonet for the 7.62mm FAL Assault rifle. First produced about 1953, the bayonet and rifle have been exported to several countries. The whole of the hilt metalwork has been parkerized, and a portion of the blade ricasso as well. The crossguard barrel ring has an extension designed to serve as a flash eliminator, and as this portion interferes with the scabbard and frog when the bayonet is sheathed, the scabbard has been deliberately made short. Thus the exposed portion of the blade had need of some protective covering. The grips are made of a dark grey, almost black, plastic composition, and are secured to the grip by means of two countersunk nuts and bolts. The blade is double-edged and has a rib traversing the centre; the upper cutting edge is slightly shorter than that on the lower edge of the blade. The scabbard is steel, and parkerized black. Attachment to the rifle is by means of a slot and spring clip and release is effected by withdrawal of the clip by means of the looped release catch situated in the pommel. *S & G Arms*

263. The Armalite AR 10 assault rifle bayonet. Originally issued to the Soudanese in 1957, the bayonet design is based on the World War II German prototype Kar 98 bayonet. The whole hilt of the bayonet is anodised a brown colour with the blade parkerized blue. (Comparison between this illustration and that of the prototype Kar 98 will display numerous distinctions.) The hilt contains a combination knife, containing penknife, screwdriver, corkscrew etc., which folds up and fits within the grip. Suspension to the belt is by means of a metal-loop frog. Blade length 7⅛″: overall length 13⅛″. *R. D. C. Evans*

261

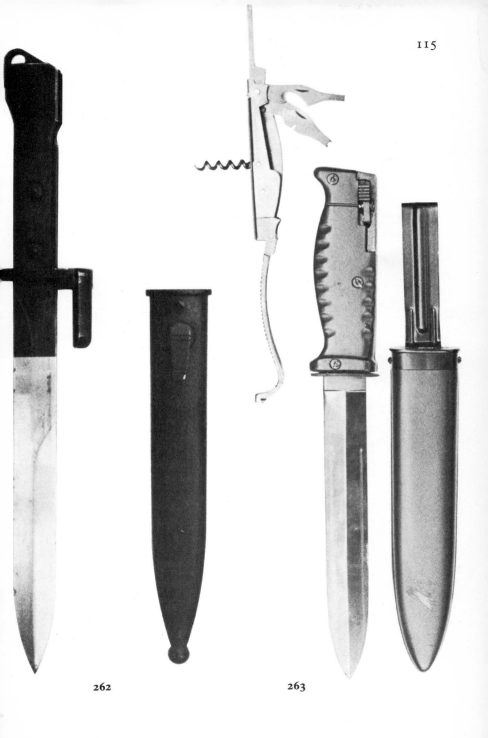

262

263

264

264. A Czechoslovakian bayonet for the Model 58 rifle (1958). A number of features makes this knife bayonet unusual and quite distinctive from other East European types. The grip is constructed of resin-bonded wood, secured to the tang by a countersunk rivet. The cross-guard and rifle slot are combined, with a press stud and locking spring integral within the crossguard. No muzzle ring exists on this bayonet, as the manner of fixing requires the bayonet to be mated with the lug from the front of the bayonet, that is to say, the bayonet is fixed by pushing along the barrel *away* from the stock. The steel blade is single edged, and fullered, with complete parkerizing. Unlike more conventional patterns of blade making, which are generally drop forged, the blade of this piece is cast by the lost wax process, and then tempered. The scabbard is made of leather, and has the frog combined with the scabbard throat. Blade length $6\frac{7}{8}''$: overall length $11\frac{1}{8}''$. *H. Haslem*

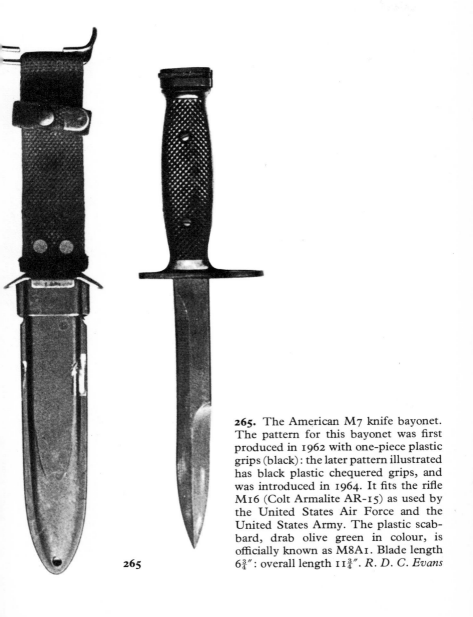

265

265. The American M7 knife bayonet. The pattern for this bayonet was first produced in 1962 with one-piece plastic grips (black): the later pattern illustrated has black plastic chequered grips, and was introduced in 1964. It fits the rifle M16 (Colt Armalite AR-15) as used by the United States Air Force and the United States Army. The plastic scabbard, drab olive green in colour, is officially known as M8A1. Blade length 6¾": overall length 11¾". *R. D. C. Evans*

▲ 266 ▼ 268

▲ 267 ▼ 269

The bayonet in wear

266. Members of the Guard, West India Regiment, Kingston, Jamaica, with Pattern 1876 Martini-Henry bayonets. Photographs detailed from picture postcard, *c.* 1890. *F. J. Stephens*

267. Troops of the Victorian Mounted Rifles, armed with Martini-Henry rifles and modified Enfield sabre bayonets. This illustration illustration is taken from a postcard, *c.* 1900. *F. J. Stephens*

268. A Lee-Metford bayonet, Pattern 1888 Mk. II, shown in wear. *Ken Holdich*

269. A Belgian Soldier of World War I, armed with an M1889 (Mauser) rifle and bayonet and also equipped with transport.

▲ **270**

270. A British soldier during World War I, posing with a captured German Uhlan (Lancer's) helmet. The bayonet in wear is a Lee-Enfield, Pattern 1888 Mk. II. *F. J. Stephens*

271. Some Dutch troops with fixed bayonets taking aim from a trench. The bayonets shown here are the long pattern (14⅛″ blade) Mannlicher rifle bayonets, Model 1895; from an unidentified Dutch magazine clipping.

▲ **271**

▲ 272

▲ 275

▲ 273

▲ 276

▲ 274

▲ 277

▲278 ▲279

272. Waffen-SS troops with fixed bayonets. The bayonets seen in this illustration can be clearly identified as being of composite grip Gew. 98 pattern. *Hugh Page Taylor*

273. German Army troops in Norway; note the World War I steel helmet worn by the soldier on the righ (modified with the Wehrmacht eagle and swastika), armed with a Steyr-Solothurn submachine-gun and a bayonet. The photo was taken from a war-time German *Signal* magazine, date unknown.

274. Two German Army personnel watching the shelling of a village. A wood grip version of the Gew. 98 bayonet can be clearly seen in wear. *Brian L. Davis*

275. Exiled members of the Free French in England during World War II. These Marine Commandos are shown equipped with No. 1 Mk. I bayonets fixed to their SMLE Mark III rifles. *The War's Best Photographs*

276. Three Dutch East Indies troops manning an anti-tank gun. The trooper on the right wears a Model 1895 Carbine bayonet. Photo taken from an unidentified Dutch magazine.

277. Two German soldiers inspecting captured arms. Note the Russian Mosin-Nagant M1891 rifles and bayonets. The photograph was taken from unidentified war-time Dutch magazine.

278. A Soviet Russian soldier seen firing a 7.62mm SKS1946 semi-automatic carbine with the folding knife bayonet shown in the 'fixed' or extended position. *U.S. Army photograph*

279. A group of Soviet Russian Army troops presenting arms. The soldiers are equipped with 7.62mm Avtomat Kalashnikob automatic rifles and carry the bayonets of the belt. *U.S. Army photograph*

280. British Troops pictured *c.* 1950 carrying old and new rifles. The soldier on the right is carrying the Rifle No. 4 with a No. 4 Mk. II* spike bayonet; the soldier on the left carries the experimental issue EM2 semi-automatic rifle with a bayonet of No. 7 type fixed

▲280

Parkerization and other preservatives

Parkerizing is a metal finishing process which affords a protective rust-preventative finish to metal work, and was first adopted by Britain about 1946.

In the past a number of methods of preserving steel have been tried, as it was noticed that, under service conditions arms carried in the field were soon exposed to a combination of maltreatment, the elements and other conditions which would, in peacetime, be classified as severe neglect.

In an attempt to stave off the effects of lack of care, unavoidable though it was, one of the first methods tried entailed the heating to red heat of the steel portions of weapons and then quickly cooling by sudden immersion in oil. The result of this 'blueing' was that the metal parts thus treated lost the gleaming surface of clean steel and became blue in colour. This blue coating, however, afforded some protection from corrosion by rust, but tended to wear off and scratch easily.

An improved method of treatment came about when the technique of 'browning' was perfected, and this was used successfully for many years. It still is used in some cases for the treatment of gun barrels. Although browning has been found to be hard wearing and long lasting it also has the disadvantage that it takes a long time to perfect—usually about five days. When the treatment of large quantities of metal parts was required this process proved, in most cases, to be highly expensive and too time consuming.

The perfection of a new method, Parkerizing, proved to have numerous advantages over the browning process and, although it is not generally considered to be as hard wearing as browning, it does have the advantage of being quick to apply, economical and usually attainable in one day's treatment.

I quote here from the pamphlet *Metal finishing processes, Parkerizing*, published by The Pyrene Company Ltd.

'Parkerizing is a two-stage rustproofing process which is applied by immersion. In the first stage the ferrous metal surface is converted into a non-metallic crystalline phosphate coating which is integral with the base metal. This highly absorbent surface, in the second stage, is impregnated with a suitable organic finishing medium. Together, the two provide a highly effective defence against corrosion.'

A number of finishes can be effected by the Parkerizing process, depending on the purpose for which the object is destined. If necessary, treated parts can be over-painted to give further protection to the parkerized finish, which can be made as 'oiled or dry, matt or glossy'.

The process of Parkerizing is not usually discussed in works devoted to bayonet collecting, but for those collectors who feel such information is useful I shall give brief details here, as outlined in the Pyrene pamphlet: *Cleaning*—firstly all the components to be treated must be cleaned thoroughly and made free from rust, dirt, grease etc. Next the cleaned components are immersed in the Parkerizing solution at a temperature suitable for the finish required. When this process has been completed, the parts are removed from the Parkerizing tank and thoroughly rinsed in clean water, which is maintained at a temperature of 170°F. If the Parkerized finish is to be painted afterwards, a small amount of chromic acid is used in a second rinse after the preliminary water rinse. Following the rinse, the metal parts are then dried off by an air blast, an oven or a hot plate as applicable. Finally the dried components are treated with an impregnation of Parker finish, or if required, with paint.

Manufacturer's markings

Shown on the opposite page are just a few of the many and varied manufacturers' markings that can be found on bayonets and knives. The key to these is as follows:

First row. Two unidentified American marks; the mark of the Pal Manufacturing Company, and that of the Union Fork and Hoe Company.

Second row. Three more unidentified American markings, and the marks of Springfield Armory and the Rock Island Armory.

Third row. The Royal cyphers of Victoria (reigned 1837–1901), George V and VI (reigned 1910–1936 and 1936–1952 respectively) and the cypher used on weapons of Indian manufacture in the period 1910–1947. The GRI represents Georgius Rex Imperator.

Fourth row. Various service acceptance markings—those of Canada, Union of South Africa, Australia (post-1900) and New Zealand. Then the 'Broad Arrow' denoting Government ownership, the 'drill purpose' mark and the Royal Navy's acceptance mark.

Fifth row. The mark of the United East India Company, used until c. 1820. Then the manufacturers' marks of Enfield Lock, the Wilkinson Sword Company and the Remington Arms Company.

Sixth row. Sundry marks: an unidentified German mark, the Nazi 'Waffenamt' marking, and two Czechoslovak marks.

AFH
U●S
1942

OL
U●S
1941

PA
U●S
1942

UFH
U●S
1943

WT
U●S
1943

UC
U●S
1943

US

SA
1906

RIA
1917

V.R.

G.R.

GRI

C U D

NAZ

DAP

N

EFD

WSC

REMINGTON

KS G

WaA 813

S

ČSZ
T

Bibliography

Akerman, John Y. 'Notes on the Origin and History of the Bayonet', *Archaeologia*. London, 1861.

Anon. 'The Bayonet, A Short Historic Sketch', *Colburn's United Services Magazine*. London, 1867.

Anon. *Organizationsbuch der NSDAP*. Munich, 1934–43.

Atwood, Major James P. *The Daggers and Edged Weapons of Hitler's Germany*. Berlin, 1965.

Blair, Claude. *European and American Arms, c. 1100–1850*. London, 1962.

Blackmore, Howard L. *British Military Firearms, 1650–1850*. London, 1961.

Guns and Rifles of the World. London, 1965.

Bozich, Stan. *German Relics, 1929–1945*. Michigan, 1967.

Burton, R. F. *A Complete System of Bayonet Exercise*. London, 1853.

Buttin, C. 'Les Baionettes', *Bulletin de la Société des Amis du Musée de l'Armée*. Paris, 1935.

Carter, J. Anthony. 'Bayonets', a continuing series of articles in *Guns Review* commencing October 1965.

Allied Bayonets of World War II. London, 1969.

Cole, Howard M. *U.S. Military Knives*. Alabama, 1968.

Coombes, J. E. and Aney, Captain J. L. *German Mauser Rifle, Model 1898*. New York, 1921 and various reprints. This booklet is generally known under the title *Gew.98*. Published by Francis Bannerman & Sons, the author's names are almost unknown.

Churchill, John, Duke of Marlborough, *The Duke of Marlborough's Exercise of Firelocks and Bayonets*. London, 1712.

Dangré, Charles. 'La Bayonette Outil' (Tool Bayonets), *Carnet de la Fourragère*. Bruxelles, 1924.

'Bayonettes Ersatz Allemandes', *Carnet de la Fourragère*. Bruxelles, 1924–32.

Eickhorn, Carl, Waffenfabrik. *Eickhorn Kundendienst* (sales catalogue). Solingen, 1939.

ffoulkes, Charles. *Arms and Armament*. London, 1945.

and Hopkinson, E. C. *Sword, Lance and Bayonet*. Cambridge, 1938: reprinted London and New York, 1967.

Hardin, Albert N., Jr. *The American Bayonet, 1776–1964*. Pennsylvania, 1964.

Holler, F. W., A.G. Edged weapon sales catalogue. Solingen, 1939.

Hutton, Alfred. *Fixed Bayonets: a Complete system of fence for the British Magazine Rifle*. London, 1890.

McGuffie, T. H. 'The Bayonet', *History Today*. London, 1962.
Maeurer, Herman A. *Military Edged Weapons of the World*. New York, 1968.
Neumann, George C. *The History of the Weapons of the American Revolution*. New York, 1967.
Raidl, R. R. and Leslie, D. R. *A Reference on Nazi Daggers and Dress Bayonets*. Cleveland, 1959.
Roads, C. H., M.A., Ph.D. *The British Soldier's Firearm, 1850–1864*. London, 1964.
Reibert, Dr. W. *Der Dienstunterricht im Heere*. Berlin, 1937.
Rollin, R. V., Jr. *U.S. Sword Bayonets, 1847–1865*. Pittsburgh, 1962.
Scott, Captain Sir Sibbald David, Bart., F.S.A. 'On the History of the Bayonet', *Journal of the Royal United Service Institution*. London, 1864.
Seilheimer, Paul, A.G. Edged weapons sales catalogue. Solingen, 1939.
Seitz, Heribert. *Blankwaffen*. Two volumes. Braunschweig, 1965 (Vol. I) and 1967 (Vol. II)
Stephens, Frederick J. *A Guide to Nazi Daggers, Swords and Bayonets*. Bury, 1965.
Bayonets—an illustrated History and Reference Guide. London 1968, revised 1968.
Theirbach, M. 'Über die Entwicklung des bajonetts', *Zeitschrift für Historische Waffenkunde*. 1900–02.
Thimm, Carl A. *A Complete Bibliography of Fencing and Duelling*. London, 1891.
Walsh, Bert. *162 Bayonets Illustrated*. Dublin, 1970.
Walter, John D. and Hughes, Gordon A. *A Primer of World Bayonets. Part I, Common Knife and Sabre Bayonets*. Brighton, 1969.
A Primer of World Bayonets. Part II, further Knife, Sabre and Socket Bayonets. Brighton, 1969.
Webster, Donald B. *American Socket Bayonets, 1717–1873*. Ottawa, 1964.
White, Major A. C. T. 'An Early Experiment in Bayonet Fighting', *The Journal of the Society for Army Historical Research*. London, 1931.
Wilkinson, Frederick. *Swords and Daggers*. London, 1967.
Wilkinson-Latham, Robert J. *British Military Bayonets, 1700–1945*. London, 1967, New York, 1968.
Various articles in *Guns Review*, commencing 1969.
WKC Stahl- und Eisenwarenfabrik G.m.b.H. Sales catalogue. Solingen, 1939.